1,000,000 Books

are available to read at

www.ForgottenBooks.com

Read online
Download PDF
Purchase in print

ISBN 978-1-333-49731-6
PIBN 10511866

This book is a reproduction of an important historical work. Forgotten Books uses state-of-the-art technology to digitally reconstruct the work, preserving the original format whilst repairing imperfections present in the aged copy. In rare cases, an imperfection in the original, such as a blemish or missing page, may be replicated in our edition. We do, however, repair the vast majority of imperfections successfully; any imperfections that remain are intentionally left to preserve the state of such historical works.

Forgotten Books is a registered trademark of FB &c Ltd.
Copyright © 2018 FB &c Ltd.
FB &c Ltd, Dalton House, 60 Windsor Avenue, London, SW19 2RR.
Company number 08720141. Registered in England and Wales.

For support please visit www.forgottenbooks.com

1 MONTH OF FREE READING

at
www.ForgottenBooks.com

By purchasing this book you are eligible for one month membership to ForgottenBooks.com, giving you unlimited access to our entire collection of over 1,000,000 titles via our web site and mobile apps.

To claim your free month visit:
www.forgottenbooks.com/free511866

* Offer is valid for 45 days from date of purchase. Terms and conditions apply.

English
Français
Deutsche
Italiano
Español
Português

www.forgottenbooks.com

Mythology Photography **Fiction** Fishing Christianity **Art** Cooking Essays **Buddhism** Freemasonry Medicine **Biology** Music **Ancient Egypt** Evolution Carpentry Physics Dance Geology **Mathematics** Fitness Shakespeare **Folklore** Yoga Marketing **Confidence** Immortality Biographies Poetry **Psychology** Witchcraft Electronics Chemistry History **Law** Accounting **Philosophy** Anthropology Alchemy Drama Quantum Mechanics Atheism Sexual Health **Ancient History** **Entrepreneurship** Languages Sport Paleontology Needlework Islam **Metaphysics** Investment Archaeology Parenting Statistics Criminology **Motivational**

A

ROLL OF ARMS

OF THE REIGN OF

RICHARD THE SECOND.

EDITED BY

THOMAS WILLEMENT,

FELLOW OF THE SOCIETY OF ANTIQUARIES.

LONDON:

WILLIAM PICKERING.

MDCCCXXXIV.

TO

HENRY FIENNES PELHAM CLINTON,

DUKE OF NEWCASTLE,

EARL OF LINCOLN,

KNIGHT OF THE MOST NOBLE ORDER OF THE GARTER,

&c. &c. &c.

THIS TRACT

IS WITH THE HIGHEST RESPECT DEDICATED

BY

His Grace's

MUCH OBLIGED AND VERY HUMBLE SERVANT,

THOMAS WILLEMENT.

PREFACE.

EVERY one who is interested in Heraldic and Genealogical inquiries, must be sensible of the deficiency of *contemporary* Records of the Arms of the Nobility and Gentry of this country in the thirteenth, fourteenth, and fifteenth centuries. With the exception of seals, paintings on glass in churches, and graphic representations on monuments and in ancient mansions, the only contemporary evidences of Arms which are preserved, consist of a few ROLLS OF ARMS, which were either compiled by the Heralds, or dictated from the recollection of some veteran knight who served in the battles of Cressy, Poictiers, and Najara, or in the glorious campaigns under the Black Prince and John of Gant, for the use of his children or friends.* A knowledge of Coat Armour was at that period an indispensible qualification for the tournament and the field ;† and it is recorded that King Edward the Third

---

* See the Scrope and Grosvenor Roll, *passim*.   † Ibid.

himself was eminently distinguished by his information on this subject.*

As examples of the general interest that prevailed about Coat Armour in the reigns of Edward the Third and Richard the Second, it is sufficient to refer to the various trials which took place before the Constable and Marshal, for the right to Armorial ensigns which were presumed to have been usurped; and more especially to the memorable controversy between Richard Lord Scrope of Bolton, and Sir Robert Grosvenor, which lasted from the year 1385, to the year 1390, the proceedings in which have been recently printed.

Though several ROLLS OF ARMS are presumed to be extant, very few have been published,† and in adding another to

---

* See preceding Note.

† The following is a correct list of Rolls alluded to:

" Roll of Arms of the reign of Henry the Third, Anno. 1240-1245."—" Roll of Arms of the reign of Edward the Second, Anno. 1308-1314."—" Roll of Arms of the reign of Edward the Third, Anno. 1337-1350."—8vos. 1828 and 1829: and the " Siege of Caerlaverock," containing the Arms of above one hundred Peers and Knights at the commencement of the fourteenth century: 4to. 1828: edited by Sir Harris Nicolas.—Pickering, Chancery-lane.

" The Heraldic Notices of Canterbury Cathedral," by the editor of this

those which have appeared, an acceptable service will it is hoped be rendered to Antiquarian literature.

In the prefaces to the publications alluded to, the value of such Rolls in illustration of Heraldry as a science, has been so fully urged, that is unnecessary to insist upon their claims to attention on this ground; and though their importance as evidence of the identity of individuals is likewise pointed out, a few sentences may be submitted in corroboration of what is there said.

Before the following sheets were sent to press, the Names and Arms of such persons mentioned therein as occur among the witnesses in the Scrope and Grosvenor controversy, were extracted for the use of the editor of the Scrope and Grosvenor Roll, to whom they proved extremely useful, not only in supplying the Arms of many of the deponents, but in identifying the families to which those individuals belonged. One or two other instances of the utility of this document, will tend to raise the value of Rolls of Arms in the estimation of

Tract, contains the blazons of many hundred Shields of Arms which were erected in that church in the reigns of Henry the Fourth, Fifth, and Sixth.

those who entertain a contemptible opinion of Heraldic pursuits; and at the same time undoubtedly fix the period at which this Roll was originally compiled.

Among the deponents in favor of Lord Scrope were "Sir Richard Abberbury," and "Sir Richard Abberbury the son," of whose lineage and arms nothing certain was known. This Roll contains the names of both these persons, and distinguishes the Arms of one of them as bearing the usual mark of filiation, a label of three points. In several cases, scarcely any other notice of the witnesses for Lord Scrope could be found, than of their Arms in this Roll; whilst of others, though various facts were collected, it presented the only satisfactory proof which could be discovered of their Armorial ensigns. Of numerous members of the Scrope family who were mentioned as cadets of the different branches of that house, the Arms of the greater part are here recorded with their respective marks of cadency. Another instance of the Arms of individuals who lived in the fourteenth century occurring in this Roll, of which no other contemporary evidence perhaps exists, is that of Sir Diggory Sees, a foreigner, who is often mentioned in the records of that period. The

PREFACE.

Roll is moreover extremely valuable for the minuteness with which marks of cadency are described, of which it often affords the only notice now extant.

These facts seem clearly to prove that this Roll was compiled towards the end of the reign of Richard the Second; but there are other circumstances which place the point beyond the possibility of being successfully controverted. With the exception of the first founders of the Order of the Garter, whose Arms extend to No. 25, which occur in a separate membrane, and which did not it is imagined form part of the original compilation, nearly if not all the persons mentioned in the Roll, flourished in the reign of Richard the Second, and the deaths of many of them in that reign, or soon after the accession of Henry the Fourth, are proved by Inquisitiones Post Mortem.

The editor is sensible that the names of Lord Botetourt, (No. 76,) who died in 1385, and Lord Beauchamp of Somerset, (No. 72,) who died in 1360, occur, though they died a few years before the period to which he has assigned the date of this compilation; but these facts may be attributed to the compiler's being forgetful or ignorant of their decease, or to his belief that they had left heirs who succeeded to their titles; and this is the more likely, as their *baptismal* names are not mentioned. The only statement of which the editor is aware, calculated to create the opinion that the Roll was compiled subsequently to the year 1397, is that Lord Lovel and Holand is said to *quarter* the arms of Lovel, (No. 62,) whereas according to modern usage, the arms of Holand should have occurred on an escutcheon of pretence, he having married the heiress of Lord Holand: but the practice of placing the arms of an heiress in an escutcheon of pretence, was not then general, even if it was ever done; and as Lord Lovel assumed the title of Holand in right of his wife, it is extremely probable that he quartered her arms with his own.

The date of the compilation may however, from the following circumstances, be more closely fixed; and they tend to place it between the years 1392 and 1397.

" Sir William Scrope " (No. 142,) was made Earl of Wiltshire on the 29th September, 1397, and his paternal Arms are given, quarterly with those of the Isle of Man, in consequence of his having in the 16 Ric. II, 1392, purchased the lordship of that island from the Earl of Salisbury. The Earl of Salisbury however appears to have retained the Arms and title of Lord of Man: and the white label over them in the Arms of Sir William Scrope was possibly introduced in consequence of an agreement with the Earl of Salisbury, as an acknowledgment of the Earl's superior and hereditary pretensions.

"The Earl of Kent" (No. 34,) was created Duke of Surrey on the 29th September, 1397.

"The Earl of Huntingdon" (No. 36,) was made Duke of Exeter on the 29th September, 1397.

"Sir Thomas Percy" (No. 80,) was created Earl of Worcester on the 29th September, 1397.

The arms attributed to Sir John Beaufort, the eldest son of John of Gant, Duke of Lancaster, by Katharine Swynford, (No. 134,) not only fix the date of this Roll to some time before the year 1397, but they establish a curious fact connected with that personage. It is stated by Sandford,* that the arms of Sir John Beaufort, before his legitimation, were those which are here assigned to him, namely, "Per pale, argent and Azure: on a bend gules, three lions passant gardant in pale Or, surmounted by a label of three points Azure, charged with nine fleurs de lis Or," being derived from the colours of the livery of the House of Lancaster, white and blue,† having on a bend, the arms of England, and the label of France, which was latterly used by John of Gant his father. The seals of John Beaufort, as Earl of Somerset, to which dignity he was raised on the 29th September, 1397, contain the entire arms of his father, viz: France and England Quarterly, within a bordure gobony Argent and Azure, which confirms the hypothesis,‡ that when he was legitimated in September 1397, he became entitled to the coat armour of his father, and discontinued the bearings which were assigned to him whilst he laboured under the stigma of bastardy.

Although the evidence that this Roll was originally com-

* Sandford's Genealogical History, where it is said that these Arms occurred in the window of Wanlip Church, in Leicestershire.
† Regal Heraldry, p. 43.   ‡ Sandford's Genealogical History.

piled in the reign of Richard the Second is conclusive, it is not pretended that the Roll from which these descriptions of the Arms are taken is of that period. On the contrary, the style of drawing and the writing appear to be much later, and bear so close a resemblance to the Roll of the Arms of the Peers who sat in Parliament in February, 6 Hen. VIII., 1515, of which a fac-simile has been published by the editor of this tract, as to justify the opinion that it was executed about that time. The frontispiece presents a fac-simile of nine of the shields taken from different parts of this Roll, which contains altogether six hundred and one shields.

Neither the genuineness as a contemporary compilation, nor the accuracy of the first membrane containing the Arms of the twenty-five founders of the Order of the Garter is insisted upon, and it is extremely doubtful if it belonged to the Roll in its original form; but it is confidently presumed that the more critically the other parts of this document are investigated, the more fully will its pretensions to be received as a correct copy of a contemporary record of the Arms of above five hundred and seventy of the Peers, Bannerets and Knights, who lived towards the close of the fifteenth century, be established. If this be conceded, the utility of these sheets, as a continuation of the series of ROLLS OF ARMS which have been given to the public, must be sufficiently evident to the Herald, the Genealogist, and the Antiquary, to justify its publication.

The original illuminated Roll, from which the following Arms have been blazoned, is now in the valuable Heraldic Library of the Rev. Canon Newling, at Litchfield, who very kindly lent it to the Editor for the purpose of publication, and to whom he offers his best acknowledgments.

1st *January*, 1834.

FROM AN ANCIENT ROLL OF ARMS,

EMBLAZONED ON VELLUM;

NOW IN THE POSSESSION OF THE REV. J. NEWLING, B.D.

CANON OF LITCHFIELD.

The Shields which contain the following twenty-five Coats of Arms, are each surrounded by the Garter, inscribed with the motto, Hony soit qui mal y pense.

1. *(No name remaining.)
   Qrtly. 1 and 4, Azure, semée de lis, or.
   2 and 3, Gules, three lions passant guardant, in pale, or.

2. Le Cont de Warwick, Thomas Beacham.
   Qrtly. 1 and 4, Gules, a fess between six cross croslets, or.
   2 and 3, Checquy, or and azure, a chevron ermine.

* King Edward III.

3. *(The name torn off.)
    Or, on a cross, sable, five escalops argent.
4. Le Cont de Stafford, Thomas Stafford.
    Or, a chevron, gules.
5. Le Cont de Salisbury, William Montacute.
    Qrtly. 1 and 4, Argent, three fusils in fess, gules.
            2 and 3, Gules, three armed legs, embowed and conjoined at the thighs, argent, garnished or.
6. Le Cont de Marche, Roger Mortimer.
    Barry of six, or and azure, on a chief of the first, three pallets between two girons of the second, based to the dexter and sinister; an escutcheon argent.
7. Monsr. John Lisle.
    Or, a fess between two chevrons, sable.
8. Monsr. Barthelmew Bourgheyche et Borewache.
    Gules, a lion rampant, queue forchée, or.
9. Monsr. John Beauchamp.
    Gules, on a fess between six cross croslets, or, a mullet sable.
10. Monsr. de Mohun.
    Or, a cross engrailed, sable
11. Monsr. Hugh Courteney.
    Or, three torteaux, two and one; a label of three points, azure
12. Monsr. Thomas Holand.
    Azure, semée de lis, a lion rampant guardant argent.

* " Le Capitow de Bouch, Monsr. Piers."—Stall Plate.

13. Monsr. John Grey.
    Barry of six, argent and azure.
14. Monsr. Richard Fitz Symond.
    Argent, three escutcheons, two and one, gules.
15. Monsr. Myles Stapilton.
    Argent, a lion rampant sable, charged on the shoulder with a mullet, or.
16. Monsr. Thomas Wale.
    Argent, a cross, sable.
17. Monsr. Hugh de Wryottesley.
    Or, a bend engrailed, gules.
18. Monsr. Neel Lorryng.
    Quarterly, argent and gules, a bend engrailed, of the last.
19. Monsr. John Chandos.
    Or, a pile, gules.
20. Monsr. James d'Awdely, apres son pere.
    Gules, a fret, or.
21. Monsr. Otes Holand.
    Azure, semée de lis, a lion rampant guardant argent.
22. Monsr. Henry Em.*
    (The shield left blank.)
23. Monsr. Sansett Dabrichecourt.
    Ermine, three bars humettée, gules.
24. Monsr. Water Paveley.
    Azure, a cross patonce, or.

* Eam.

25. Le Roy Richard D'angleterre fitz du noble prince de Galles, Edw:
> Qrtly. 1 and 4, Azure, three fleurs de lis, or.
>> 2 and 3, Gules, three lions passant guardant, in pale, or.

(The last Shield is placed in the centre of the Vellum, and concludes those surrounded by the Garter. The Shields following are placed six in each line, with the names above.)

26. Le Duc John de Lancastre.
> Qrtly. 1 and 4, Azure, semée de lis, or.
>> 2 and 3, Gules, three lions passant guardant, in pale, or. Over all a label of three points, ermine.

27. Le Duc de Everwyke.*
> Qrtly. 1 and 4, Azure, semée de lis, or.
>> 2 and 3, Gules, three lions passant guardant, in pale, or. Over all a label of three points, each charged with as many torteaux.

28. Le Duc de Glowcestre.
> Quarterly 1, Azure, semée de lis, or.
>> 2 and 3, Gules, three lions passant guardant, or.
>> 4, Azure, a bend argent between two cottices and six lions rampant, or. A bordure argent, which only encloses the three first quarters.

29. Le Conte de Derby, Henry.
> Qrtly. 1 and 4, Azure, semée de lis, or.
>> 2 and 3, Gules, three lions passant guardant, or.

* York.

A label of five points, per pale, ermine, and azure charged with nine fleurs de lis, or.

30. Le Conte de Rutteland.

Qrtly. 1 and 4, Azure, semée de lis, or.

2 and 3, Gules, three lions passant guardant, or. A label of five points, per pale; first argent, charged with nine torteaux; second gules, charged with three castles, or.

31. Le Conte de la Marche et de Ulster.

Qrtly. 1 and 4, Azure, three bars, or, on a chief of the first, two pallets between as many girons, of the second, based dexter and sinister; an escutcheon argent.

2 and 3, Or, a cross, gules.

32. Le Conte d'Arondell et de Warren.

Qrtly. 1 and 4, Gules, a lion rampant, or.

2 and 3, Chequy, or and azure.

33. Le Conte Maryschall, Sr. de Mowbray.

Qrtly. 1 and 4, Gules, three lions passant guardant, in pale or, a label of five points argent.

2 and 3, Gules, a lion rampant argent.

34. Le Conte de Kent, Holland.

Gules, three lions passant guardant, in pale, or; a bordure argent.

35. Le Conte de Warwick, Beauchamp.

Gules, a fess between six cross croslets, or.

36. Le Conte de Huntyngdon, (*Duke de Excester, Holland.*)*
    Gules, three lions passant guardant, in pale, or; a bordure azure, charged with eight fleurs de lis, or.

37. Le Conte de Salesbury, Montague.
    Qrtly. 1 and 4, Gules, three armed legs embowed and conjoined at the thighs argent, garnished, or.
    2 and 3, Argent, three fusils in fess, gules.

38. Le Conte de Devonshyre, Courteneye.
    Or, three torteaux, two and one. A label of three points, azure.

39. Le Conte de Northumberland, Sr. de Lucy.
    Qrtly. 1 and 4, Or, a lion rampant, azure.
    2 and 3, Gules, three lucies haurient, two and one argent.

40. Le Conte de Stafford.
    Or, a chevron, gules.

41. Le Conte de Oxinford.
    Quarterly, or and gules, in the dexter chief a mullet argent.

42. Le Sr. le Spenser.
    Quarterly, argent and gules; the second and third charged with a fret, or; over all a bendlet sable.

43. Le Sr. le Roos et de Badlismere.
    Qrtly. 1 and 4, Gules, three water budgets argent, two and one.
    2 and 3, Argent, a fess double cottised, gules.

---

* In a somewhat later hand.

44. Le Sr. Grey de Codnor.
   Barry of six, argent and azure.
45. Le Sr. Fitz Wa'ter.
   Or, a fess between two chevrons, gules.
46. Le Sr. le Beaumont.
   Azure, semée de lis, a lion rampant, or.
47. Le Sr. de Nevyll.
   Gules, a saltire argent.
48. Le Sr. de Clifford.
   Chequy, or and azure, a fess, gules.
49. Le Sr. la Zowche.
   Gules, bezantée, a canton ermine.
50. Le Sr. Grey de Ruyffyn.
   Barry of six, argent and azure, in chief three torteaux.
51. Le Sr. le Strange.
   Gules, two lions passant in pale, argent.
52. Le Sr. de Wyloughby.
   Qrtly. 1 and 4, Sable, a cross engrailed, or.
   2 and 3, Gules, a cross moline argent.
53. Le Sr. la Warre.
   Gules, semée of cross croslets fitchée, a lion rampant or, armed &c azure.
54. Le Sr. Darcy.
   Qrtly. 1 and 4, Azure, three cinqfoils, two and one, between eight cross croslets, argent.
   2 and 3, Azure, three bars gemels, and a chief, or.
55. Le Sr. le Scales.
   Gules, six escallops, three, two and one, argent.
56. Le Sr. le Bardolf.
   Argent, three cinqfoils, two and one, or, pierced.

57. Le Sr. de Berkele.
    Gules, a chevron between six cross croslets in chief, and four in base argent.
58. Le Sr. de Seynt Amand.
    Or, fretty sable, on a chief of the last, three bezants.
59. Le Sr. de le Lisle.
    Gules, a lion passant guardant argent, crowned, or.
60. Le Sr. de Morley.
    Argent, a lion rampant sable, crowned, or.
61. Le Sr. de Charleton.
    Or, a lion rampant, gules.
62. Le Sr. de Lovel et Holland.
    Qrtly. 1 and 4, Barry, nebulée of six, or and gules. 2 and 3, Azure, semée de lis, a lion rampant guardant, argent.
63. Le Sr. de Welles.
    Or, a lion rampant, queue forchée sable.
64. Le Sr. le Grey de Rotherfeld.
    Barry of six, argent and azure, a bend, gules.
65. Le Sr. de Cobham.
    Gules on a chevron, or, three lions rampant, sable.
66. Le Sr. le Poinynges.
    Barry of six, or and vert, a bendlet, gules.
67. Le Sr. de Ferers de Groby.
    Gules, seven mascles conjoined, three, three and one, or.
68. Le Sr. de Harynton.
    Sable, a fret argent.

69. Le Sr. le Seint John.
　　Argent, on a chief, gules, two mullets of six points or, pierced azure.
70. Le Sr. le Burnel.
　　Argent, a lion rampant sable, crowned or; a bordure azure.
71. Monsr. Ric. Talbot.
　　Qrtly. 1 and 4, Gules, a lion rampant, within a bordure engrailed, or.
　　2 and 3, Argent, two lions passant, in pale, gules.*
72. Le Sr. le Beauchamp de Som's.
　　Vaire argent and azure.
73. Le Sr. le Bousers.
　　Argent, a cross engrailed gules, between four water budgets, sable.
74. Le Sr. le Deyncourte.
　　Azure, a fess dancettée between four billets in chief, and six in base, or.
75. Le Sr. de Dacre.
　　Gules, three escalops two and one, argent.
76. Le Sr. le Botourt.
　　Or, a saltire engrailed, sable.
77. Le Sr. le Camoys.
　　Or, on a chief gules, three plates.
78. Le Sr. le Faukonberge.
　　Argent, a lion rampant, azure.

* Vide Frontispiece.

79. Monsr. Thos Moubray.
   Qrtly. 1 and 4, Gules, three lions passant gaurdant, in pale, or; a label of three points, argent, charged with three eagles displayed, of the first.
   2 and 3, Gules, a lion rampant, or, a label of three points azure.
80. Monsr. Thos. Percy.
   Or, a lion rampant, azure.
81. Monsr. Henry Percy.
   Or, a lion rampant azure, a label of three points, gules.
82. Monsr. Henr. le Skrop.
   Azure, a bend, or; a label of three points, argent.
83. Monsr. William Beuchamp.
   Gules, on a fess between six cross croslets, or, a crescent sable.
84. Monsr. Heugh de Calv'ley.
   Argent, a fess gules between three calves, sable.
85. Monsr. Hugh la Zouche.
   Gules, ten bezants; four, three, two and one.
86. Monsr. Philip Spencer.
   Barry of six, or and azure, a canton ermine.
87. Monsr. Reynold de Ev'yngham.
   Qrtly. 1 and 4, Gules, a lion rampant vaire.
   2 and 3, Sable, a bend between six cross croslets, argent.
88. Le Baron de Greystok.
   Barry of sixteen, argent and azure, three chaplets two and one, gules.

89. Monsr. William Botrewe.
    Argent, a griffon segreant gules, armed azure.
90. Monsr. Guy de Bryan.
    Or, three piles from the chief, azure.
91. Monsr. John Montagu.
    Argent, three fusils in fess gules, a bordure sable.
92. Le Sr. de Astle.
    Azure, a cinqfoil ermine, pierced.
93. Monsr. Raynold de Cobham.
    Gules on a chevron, or, three estoiles sable.
94. Le Sr. de Ferrers.
    Vaire or and gules.
95. Monsr. Deggar Sees.
    Per fess, or and azure, in chief a demi lion rampant issuant sable, in base six plates, three, two and one.
96. Monsr. Rauf Hastynges.
    Argent, a manche sable.
97. Le Baron de Hilton.
    Argent, two bars azure.
98. Monsr. John Deverose.
    Argent, on a fess gules, a mullet or, in chief three torteaux.
99. Monsr. Richard le Skrop.
    Azure, a bend or.
100. Monsr. Rauf Lumleye.
    Argent, a fess gules, between three popinjays proper.

101. Monsr. John de Clynton.
Argent, on a chief azure, two mullets of six points, or, pierced gules.*

102. Monsr. Robert Knolles.
Gules, on a chevron argent, three roses of the field.

103. Monsr. E'mond de Stafford. [*Clerk.*]
Or, a chevron gules, between three martlets sable.

104. Monsr. Mays Gournay.
Paly of six, or and azure.

105. Monsr. Rauf Bulmer.
Gules, billettée, a lion rampant, or.

106. Monsr. Aubry le Vere.
Quarterly gules and or, in the dexter chief a mullet, ermine.

107. Monsr. Philip Courtney.
Or, three torteaux, two and one; on a label of three points azure, nine plates.

108. Monsr. William Nevill.
Gules on a saltire argent, a fleur de lis azure.

109. Monsr. Henry Grey de Wilton.
Barry of six, argent and azure, a label of five points, gules.

110. Monsr. Rauf Cromwell, le Sr. de Tatirsale.
Qrtly. 1 and 4, Chequy or and gules, a chief ermine.
2 and 3, Argent, a chief gules, surmounted by a bend sable.

* Vide Frontispiece.

111. Monsr. Ric. Norlande.
Sable, a chevron between three wolves' heads, argent, couped gules.
112. Monsr. Mays Redmane.
Gules, a chevron argent, between three lozenge cushions, ermine, tassled or.
113. Monsr. Bryan de Stapelton.
Argent, a lion rampant, sable, charged on the shoulder with a mullet, gules, pierced.
114. Monsr. Baudewyn Frevill.
Or, a cross patonce, gules.
115. Monsr. Lewys de Clyfford.
Chequy, or and azure, a fess and bordure, gules.
116. Monsr. Thomas Gray.
Gules, a lion rampant within a bordure engrailed, argent.
117. Monsr. Rauf de Euar.
Quarterly or and gules, on a bend sable, three escalops argent.
118. Monsr. Thomas Colpeper.
Qrtly. 1 and 4, Argent, a chevron sable between five martlets in chief and two in base, gules.
2 and 3, Argent, a bend engrailed, gules.
119. Monsr. William de Cosyngton.
Azure, three roses, two and one, or.
120. Monsr. Miles de Stapulton.
Argent, a lion rampant, sable.

121. Monsr. Thomas de Metham.
 Quarterly azure and argent, in the dexter chief a fleur de lis, or.
122. Monsr. Thomas Talbott.
 Argent, three lions rampant, two and one purpure.
123. Monsr. Thomas Fitz Simonde.
 Or, a chief gules.
124. Monsr Rauff Percy.
 Or, a lion rampant, azure, charged on the shoulder with a mullet of the field.
125. Monsr. Hugh le Spencer.
 Quarterly argent, and gules frettée or, over all a bendlet sable; in chief of the first quarter, a martlet of the last.
126. Monsr. Robert de Clifford.
 Chequy or and azure, on a fess gules, a crescent, or.
127. Monsr. William le Roos.
 Gules, three water budgets, two and one, argent; the first charged with a crescent, sable.
128. Monsr. William le Bryan.
 Or, three piles from the chief, azure; a canton paly of four, argent and azure, charged with a bend gules, thereon three eagles displayed, or.
129. Monsr. Barthelmew Bousers.
 Argent, a cross engrailed, gules, between four water budgets, sable, a label of three points, azure.
130. Monsr. Mihell de la Poole.
 Azure, a fess between three leopards' faces, or.

131. Monsr. Bawdwyn Beresforde.
   Argent, three fleurs de lis, two and one, between six cross croslets, fitchée, sable.
132. Monsr. Thomas Harecourte.
   Or, two bars, gules.
133. Monsr. Roger de Clarendon.
   Gules, a bend, or.
134. Monsr. John Beaufort.
   Per pale, argent and azure; on a bend gules, three lions passant guardant, in pale, or, surmounted by a label of three points azure, charged with nine fleurs de lis, or.
135. Monsr. Thomas Nevill.
   Gules on a saltire, argent, a martlet of the field.
136. Monsr. Thomas le Scrop.
   Azure, a bend or, a label of three points argent, charged with an annulet, sable.
137. Monsr. .... Fitz Waryn.
   Quarterly per fess indentée, argent and gules.
138. Monsr. Henry Fitz Hugh.
   Azure, three chevrons interlaced, and a chief, or.
139. Monsr. Robert Nevill.
   Argent, a saltire, gules.
140. Monsr. Ric. de Houghton.
   Sable, three bars, argent.
141. Monsr. .... Fitz Waryu.
   Quarterly per fess indentée, ermine and gules.

142. Monsr. William le Scrop.

 Qrtly. 1 and 4, Gules, three armed legs, embowed and conjoined at the thighs, argent, garnished or; a label of three points, argent.

 2 and 3, Azure, a bend or, a label of three points, gules.*

143. Monsr. Gérard de Braybrok.

 Argent, seven mascles, three, three and one, gules.

144. Monsr. John le Scrop.

 Azure, a bend, or, a label of three points, ermine.

145. Monsr. Thomas Latymer.

 Gules, a cross patonce, or, a label of three points, azure.

146. Monsr. Henri le Scrop.

 Azure, a bend, or; a label of three points, argent, charged with as many bars, gules.

147. Monsr. John de Fallesle.

 Or, two chevrons, gules.

148. Monsr. .... le Scrop.

 Azure, a bend or, charged in chief with a lozenge ermine.

149. Monsr. John Trayly.

 Or, a cross between four martlets, gules.

150. Monsr. Steven le Scrop.

 Azure, a bend, or, charged in chief with a mullet, ermine.

---

* Vide Frontispiece.

151. Monsr. Robert Ogyl.
 Qrtly. 1 and 4, Argent, a fess between three crescents, gules.
 2 and 3, Or, an orle azure.
152. Monsr. John Hawkewode.
 Argent, on a chevron sable, three escalops of the field.
153. Monsr. Robert Ferrers.
 Vaire or and gules.
154. Monsr. John Bussy.
 Argent, three bars sable.
155. Monsr. Richard Waldeg've.
 Per pale, argent and gules.
156. Monsr. John Deyncourt.
 Argent, a fess dancettée between four billets in chief and six in base, sable.
157. Monsr. Robert de Swyli'gton.
 Argent, a chevron azure, a label of three points ermine.
158. Monsr. John Rocheford.
 Quarterly or and gules, a bordure sable charged with eleven bezants.
159. Monsr. Rauff Rocheford.
 Quarterly or and gules, in the sinister chief an annulet argent, a bordure sable charged with ten bezants.
160. Monsr. John de Hollande.
 Azure, semée de lis, a lion rampant gaurdant, argent.
161. Monsr. Robert Marny.
 Gules, a lion rampant gaurdant, argent.

162. Monsr. Bernard Brokas.
    Sable, a lion rampant gaurdant, or.
163. Monsr. Willm. Marny.
    Gules, a lion rampant gaurdant argent, a label of three points, or.
164. Monsr. Adam Franceis.
    Per bend sinister, sable and or, a lion rampant counterchanged.
165. Monsr. John Colvyle.
    Azure, a lion rampant argent.
166. Monsr. John Peeche.
    Azure, a lion rampant queue forchée ermine, crowned or.
167. Mons. John Atte Wode.
    Gules, a lion rampant queue forchée argent.
168. Monsr. James Bellers.
    Per pale, gules and sable, a lion rampant argent.
169. Monsr. Henry de Heton.
    Azure, a lion rampant argent.
170. Monsr. Robert ....
    Ermine, a lion rampant azure.
171. Monsr. James le Pykeryng.
    Ermine, a lion rampant azure.*
172. Monsr. Bawdwyn Seint George.
    Per fess azure and argent, over all a lion rampant gules, crowned or.

* Vide Frontispiece.

173. Monsr. Simond Felbrige.
    Or, a lion rampant gules.
174. Monsr. George Felbrige.
    Or, a lion rampant gules, charged on the shoulder with a mullet argent, pierced.
175. Monsr. John Pomeray.
    Or, a lion rampant, gules, within a bordure engrailed sable.
176. Monsr, Roger Fauco'b'ge.
    Argent, a lion rampant azure, charged on the shoulder with a fleur de lis or.
177. Monsr. Thomas Mounford.
    Argent, semée of cross croslets, gules, a lion rampant azure.
178. Monsr. John Basset.
    Or, three piles from the chief, gules; on a canton argent a griffon segreant sable, armed gules.
179. Monsr. Thomas Fogge.
    Argent, on a fess between three annulets sable, as many mullets of six points, of the field, pierced.
180. Monsr. Emond Appelby.
    Azure, six martlets, three, two and one, or.
181. Monsr. Thomas Musgrave.
    Azure, six annulets, three, two and one, or.
182. Monsr. John de Annesleye.
    Paly of six, argent and azure, a bendlet gules.
183. Monsr. John Fenwik.
    Per fess gules and argent, six martlets, three, two and one, counterchanged.

184. Monsr. Umffrey de Stafford.
   Or, a chevron gules, within a bordure engrailed sable.
185. Monsr. William Moigne.
   Argent, two bars, in chief three mullets of six points sable.
186. Monsr. Nicol de Stafford.
   Or, a chevron gules, a chief azure.
187. Monsr. John de Eynesford.
   Gules, a fret ermine.
188. Monsr. Walt. Blount.
   Barry nebulée of eight, or and sable.
189. Monsr. John de Eynesford.
   Gules, a fret engrailed ermine.
190. Monsr. Thomas de Clynton.
   Argent, on a chief azure, two mullets of six points, or, pierced gules; over all a label of three points ermine.*
191. Monsr. John Hodelston.
   Gules, a fret argent.
192. Monsr. John Mardak.
   Or, a fret sable.
193. Monsr. John Verdon.
   Or, a fret gules.
194. Monsr. Nicol Hary'gton.
   Sable, a fret argent, a label of three points, gules.
195. Monsr. Avery Trussell.
   Or, a fret gules, charged with nine bezants.

* Vide Frontispiece.

196. Monsr. John Kentwode.
Gules, three roses ermine, seeded gules.
197. Monsr. Ric: Abberbury.
Or, a fess double embattled on the top, sable.
198. Monsr. Gilbert Talbott.
Gules, two bars vaire, in the dexter chief a mullet argent, pierced.
199. Monsr. Gerard Salvayn.
Argent, on a chief sable, two mullets of six points, or, pierced gules.*
200. Monsr. John Hawarde.
Gules, a bend between six cross croslets fitchée argent.†
201. Monsr. Thom. Fitz Henry.
Argent, a cross engrailed sable.
202. Monsr. Thom. de Strothere.
Gules, on a bend argent, three eagles displayed vert, armed gules.
203. Monsr. Willm. de Lyle.
Or, on a fess between two chevrons sable, a martlet of the field.
204. Monsr. John Mauers.
Or, two bars azure, a chief gules.
205. Monsr. Thom. de Herpyngh'm.
Azure, an escutcheon within an orle of eight martlets, argent.
206. Monsr. Thom. Reynes.
Chequy or and gules, a canton ermine.

* Vide Frontispiece.   † Ib.

207. Monsr. Thomas Erpingham.
   Azure, an escutcheon within an orle of eight martlets, or.
208. Monsr. Robert Swynbourne.
   Gules, semée of cross croslets, three boars' heads couped argent, armed or.
209. Monsr. Reynald Hakenbeche.
   Or, two bars azure.
210. Monsr. Thom. Swynbourne.
   Gules, semée of cross croslets, three boars' heads couped argent, a label of three points, or.
211. Monsr. Willm. a Wawton.
   Argent, a chevron sable.
212. Mons. John Predias.
   Argent, a chevron sable, a label of three points, gules.
213. Monsr. Th. de Rameston.
   Argent, a chevron sable, in the dexter chief a cinqfoil of the last, pierced.
214. Monsr. Hue Lutrel.
   Or, a bend between six martlets, within a bordure engrailed sable.
215. Monsr. R'ynard de la Beer.
   Azure, a bend cottized argent, between six martlets, or.
216. Monsr. John Mounçeneye.
   Gules, a bend between six martlets, or.
217. Monsr. Robt. Mounçeneye.
   Azure, a bend between six martlets, or.

23

218. Monsr. John de Seyton.
    Gules, a bend argent, between six martlets, or.
219. Mons. Richard Tempest.
    Argent, a bend between six martlets sable.
220. Monsr. Nicolas de Longeford.
    Paly of six, or and gules, a bendlet, argent.
221. Monsr. John Gery.
    Paly of six, or and gules, a chief ermine.
222. Monsr. John de Byrton.
    Paly of six, or and gules, on a bend sable, three water budgets argent.
223. Monsr. Robert Corbet.
    Argent, two bars and a canton, gules.
224. Monsr. Robt. son fitz.
    Argent, two bars and a canton, gules, over all a label of three points, argent.
225. Monsr. Roger le Boys.
    Argent, two bars and a canton, gules, over all a bendlet sable.
226. Monsr. Willm. de Lancastre.
    Argent, two bars gules, a quarter of the last charged with a lion passant guardant, or.
227. Monsr. Richard de Kyrkeby.
    Argent, two bars gules, on a canton of the last, a cross moline, or.
228. Monsr. John Derwentwater.
    Argent, two bars gules, on a canton of the last, a cinqfoil or, pierced.

229. Monsr. John de Thorp.
   Azure, a fess dancettée, ermine.
230. Monsr. Willm. de Pappeworth.
   Gules, a fess dancettée, argent.
231. Monsr. Willm. de Vavasore.
   Or, a fess dancettée, sable.
232. Monsr. Geffrey Lucy.
   Gules, semée of cross croslets, three lucies haurient, two and one, or.
233. Monsr. Robt. de Laton.
   Argent, on a fess between six cross croslets fitchée sable, a cinqfoil of the field, pierced.
234. Monsr. Reynald Lucy.
   Gules, semée of cross croslets, three lucies haurient two and one, or, a label of three points, azure.
235. Monsr. Thomas de Asteley.
   Azure, a cinqfoil ermine, pierced; over all a label of three points, or, charged with two bars, gules.
236. Monsr. Wau't Chaundos.
   Or, a pile from the chief, gules.
237. Monsr. Thomas de Hasteley de Morton.
   Azure, a cinqfoil ermine, pierced, within a bordure engrailed, or.
238. Monsr. Andrew de Leyke.
   Argent, a chief gules, surmounted by a bend engrailed, azure.
239. Monsr. John de Leyke.
   Argent, on a saltire engrailed sable, nine annulets, or.

240. Monsr. Robt. de Leyke.
   Argent, a chief gules, surmounted by a bend engrailed azure, in the sinister chief a mullet, or, pierced.
241. Monsr. John de Colvile.
   Argent, on a fess gules between three calves, sable, a crescent, or.
242. Monsr. John de Tiringham.
   Azure, a saltire engrailed, argent.
243. Monsr. Hue de Colvile.
   Argent, on a fess gules between three calves, sable, a mullet or.
244. Monsr. Robt. Clav'yng.
   Quarterly or and gules, a bendlet sable.
245. Mons. Willm. Fitz Will'm.
   Lozengée argent and gules.
246. Monsr. John Clav'ing.
   Quarterly or and gules, a bendlet sable, over all a label of three points argent.
247. Monsr. Robert de Clyfton.
   Sable, on a bend argent, three mullets, gules.
248. Monsr. Andrw. Lot'rel.
   Azure, a bend between six martlets, argent.
249. Monsr. Nycol de Clyfton.
   Sable, on a bend argent, three crescents gules, in the sinister chief a crescent of the second.
250. Monsr. Nicol Mongomeri.
   Or, an eagle displayed azure, beaked and legged, gules.

E

251. Monsr. John Dev'rose.
   Argent, a fess gules, in chief three torteaux.
252. Monsr. John Colvyll.
   Or, a fess gules, in chief three torteaux.
253. Monsr. James le Roos.
   Gules, three water budgets ermine, two and one.
254. Monsr. John de Aylesbury.
   Azure, a cross argent.
255. Monsr. Thomas son fitz.
   Azure, a cross argent, a label of three points, gules.
256. Monsr. Thomas Fitz Nicol.
   Quarterly gules and or, a bendlet, argent.
257. Monsr. Thomas Sakevill.
   Ermine, three chevronels, gules.
258. Monsr. Thom. Sakeville.
   Quarterly gules and or, a bend vaire.
259. Monsr. Robt. de Passele.
   Gules, a lion rampant, or.
260. Monsr. Thomas de Cobham.
   Gules, a cross argent.
261. Monsr. Willm. Bur.
   Azure, billettée, a lion rampant, or.
262. Monsr. Thomas le Roos.
   Or, three water budgets sable, two and one.
263. Monsr. Robt. le Roos.
   Azure, three water budgets or, two and one.
264. Monsr. John Lilbourne.
   Sable, three water budgets argent, two and one.

265. Monsr. Y'poffer de Langeton.
    Argent, three chevronels gules, a label of three points, azure.
266. Monsr. Willm. de Dyks.
    Argent, a fess vaire or and gules, between three water budgets, sable.
267. Monsr. Willm. Bagot.
    Argent, on a chevron gules between three martlets sable, a crescent of the field.
268. Monsr. Willm. de Melton.
    Azure, a cross patonce voided, argent.
269. Monsr. John de Wilton.
    Gules, on a chevron argent, three cross croslets fitchée of the field.
270. Monsr. Hugh de Shirleye.
    Paly of six, or and azure, a canton ermine.
271. Monsr. Thomas de Wennesley.
    Ermine, on a bend gules, three escalops or.
272. Monsr. Ric. de Goldesborow.
    Azure, a cross patonce argent.
273. Monsr. John Warde.
    Azure, a cross patonce or.
274. Monsr. Robt. Sleght.
    Or, a chevron between six cross croslets in chief, and four in base, sable.
275. Monsr. Robt. de Urswike.
    Argent, on a bend sable, three lozenges of the field, each charged mith a saltire, gules.

276. Monsr. Thom. Walshe.
   Gules, two bars gemels argent, surmounted by a bendlet of the same.
277. Monsr. Pers de Carew.
   Argent, three bars gemels, sable.
278. Monsr. Thomas Umfravill.
   Gules, crusilée a cinqfoil or, pierced.
279. Monsr. Avery Britchebury.
   Argent, two bars azure, on a canton of the last a martlet, or.
280. Monsr. Thomas Marchy'gton.
   Or, a fret sable, canton gules.
281. Monsr. John Bagot.
   Argent, a chevron gules, between three martlets sable
282. Monsr. Philipp de Oker'.
   Ermine, on a chief gules, three bezants.
283. Monsr. Hugh de Browe.
   Gules, on a chevron argent, three roses of the field, seeded or.
284. Lawrens de Dutton.
   Quarterly 1 and 4, Argent. 2 and 3, Gules, a fret or.
285. Monsr. Lawrans Evingh'm.
   Quarterly argent and sable, a bendlet of the last.
286. Monsr. Edmond Fitz Hugh.
   Gules, three lions rampant, two and one, or, a bordure engrailed, argent.
287. Monsr. John Boteler.
   Azure, a bend argent between six covered cups, or.

288. Monsr. Edward Boteler.
Gules, a fess componée, counter componée, or and sable, between six cross croslets, argent.
289. Monsr. John Boteler.
Azure, a chevron between three covered cups, or.
290. .... Tichett.
Ermine, a chevron, gules.
291. Monsr. John Burdet.
Azure, two bars or, each charged with three martlets, gules.
292. Monsr. John Dodyngsele.
Argent, a fess gules.
293. Monsr. John Soardeby.
Argent, a bend cottised between six lions rampant sable.
294. Monsr. Nicol Byllynge.
Gules, three fish naiant in pale or, a bordure engrailed, argent.
295. Monsr. Thomas de Rokeby.
Argent, a chevron sable between three rooks proper.
296. Monsr. Ric. de Beulee.
Quarterly argent and gules, a rose counterchanged, seeded or.
297. Monsr. Willm. Saly.
Quarterly argent and sable, a bendlet gules.
298. Monsr. Thomas Cheyne.
Azure, on a fess nebulée between three crescents or, a fleur de lis, gules.

299. Monsr. Rauff Brasbrige.
   Vaire argent and sable, a fess gules.
300. Monsr. Thomas Henmale.
   Or, on a fess between two chevrons, gules, three escalops of the field.
301. Monsr. Gerrard de Grymston.
   Argent, on a fess sable, three mullets or, pierced gules.
302. Monsr. Rauff Cheyne.
   Gules, four fusils in fess argent, each charged with an escalop sable, a border of the second.
303. Monsr. Edmond de Thorp.
   Azure, three crescents argent, two and one.
304. Monsr. John de Ingesthorp.
   Gules, a cross engrailed argent.
305. Monsr. Roger Curson.
   Argent, on a bend sable, the popinjays or, collared and legged, gules; in the sinister chief a crescent of the last.
306. Monsr. Willm. Scargil.
   Ermine, a saltire gules.
307. Monsr. Godfry Foljambe.
   Sable, a bend or between six escalops, argent.
308. Thomas Pikworth.
   Argent, three pick-axes, gules, two and one.
309. Monsr. Willm. Swalow.
   Or, a fess between three swallows rising sable.
310. Monsr. Robert Picworth.
   Argent, an annulet between three pick-axes, gules.

311. Monsr. Robert Fraunceys.
Argent, a chevron between three eagles displayed, gules, armed azure.
312. Monsr. John Pekbrugge.
Or, a fess double cottised azure, a bendlet gules.
313. Monsr. John *(Bonatlem.*)*
Argent, a chevron between three crescents, gules.
314. Monsr. Steven de Hales.
Sable, a chevron between three lions rampant, argent.
315. Monsr. Rauff de Ipre.
Argent, on a chevron between three bulls' heads caboshed, gules; a mullet of the field.
316. Monsr. Thomas Southworth.
Sable, a chevron between three crosses patonce, argent.
317. Monsr. Richard de By'gham.
Or, on a fess gules, three water budgets argent.
318. Monsr. Edmond Wyloughby.
Or, two bars gules, charged with three water budgets argent, two and one.
319. *(Colvil.*)*
Or, on a fess gules, three lions rampant, argent.
320. Monsr. Nicol Dabrichcourt.
Ermine, three bars humettée, gules.
321. Monsr. Robt. de Whitneye.
Azure, a cross componée, counter componée, or and gules.

* In a somewhat later hand.

322. Monsr. John de Dabrichecourt.
Ermine, three bars humettee gules, each charged with as many escalops, or.
323. Monsr. Rauff de Shelton.
Azure, a cross or.
324. Monsr. Robt. de Rokeley.
Lozengée argent and gules, a fess sable.
325. Monsr. Rauff de Schelton.
Azure, a cross or, a label of three points argent.
326. Monsr. Rauffe Seynt Legger.
Azure, frettée argent, a chief or.
327. Monsr. Wauter Taylboys.
Argent, a saltire gules, on a chief of the last three escalops of the field.
328. Monsr Renold Seynt Leggere.
Azure, frettée argent, a chief or, in the dexter chief a mullet of six points, gules.
329. Monsr. Peris de Boughton.
Gules, a goat saliant, or.
230. Monsr. Henri de Rydford.
Argent, frettée and a chief sable.
331. Monsr. Willm. de Ermine.
Ermine, a saltire engrailed gules, on a chief of the last a lion passant gaurdant, or.
332. Monsr. Thomas Hawley.
Azure, a saltire engrailed, argent.
333. Monsr. Alisund Nevill.
Gules, on a saltire argent, a mullet sable, pierced.

334. Monsr. Willm. de Bolesby.
    Sable, a saltire or.
335. Monsr. Edmond Heng've.
    Argent, a chief dancettée, gules.
336. Monsr. Randolff Fitz John.
    Azure, a chief dancettée, or.
337. Monsr. Edward Seint John.
    Argent, on a chief dancettée, gules, two mullets of six points, or, pierced vert.
338. Monsr. Thom. Kydeley.
    Sable, a saltire embattled argent.
339. Monsr. Thom. de Boynton.
    Or, a fess between three crescents, gules.
340. Monsr. John de Grymesby.
    Per chevron sable and argent, in chief two cinqfoils of the field, pierced.
341. Monsr. John Paynell.
    Gules, two chevronels and a bordure argent
342. Monsr. Willm. de Rylliston.
    Sable, a saltire argent.
343. Monsr. Willm. Swynburne.
    Per fess gules and argent, three roses two and one, counterchanged, seeded or.
344. Monsr. Ric. Grey.
    Barry of six argent and azure, a bend gules.
345. Monsr. John de le Pole.
    Or, a stag's head caboshed, gules, between the antlers a fleur de lis of the last.

346. Monsr. Thomas Flemyng.
>Barry of six argent and azure, in chief three lozenges, gules.

347. Monsr. Edmond de Missenden.
>Or, a cross engrailed gules, in the dexter canton a crow proper.

348. Monsr. Laurens de Papenh'm.
>Barry of six argent and azure, on a bend gules, three mullets or, pierced of the second.

349. Monsr. John de Holgom.
>Or, on a bend sable, three mullets argent.

350. Monsr. John le Strange.
>Gules, two lions passant in pale argent.

351. Monsr. Thom. de Ernington.
>Azure, two lions passant in pale or.

352. Monsr. John le Straunge.
>Gules, two lions passant in pale argent, a bendlet or.

353. Monsr. Arnold Savage.
>Argent, six lions rampant, three, two and one, sable.

354. Monsr. Thomas Leybourne.
>Gules, six lions rampant, three, two and one, argent.

355. Monsr. Edmond Perpond.
>Sable, a lion rampant within an orle of cinqfoils argent.

356. Monsr. Willm. de Laton.
>Or, a cross moline, gules.

357. Monsr. Ric. Craddok.
>Argent, on a chevron azure, three garbs, or.

358. Monsr. Willm. Birlande.
   Gules, a chevron between three bears' heads couped argent, muzzled, of the field.
359. Monsr. William Goderiche.
   Argent, two lions passant guardant in pale sable.
360. Monsr. John Littelbury.
   Argent, two lions passant gaurdant in pale gules.
361. Monsr. Willm. Barre.
   Azure, two lions passant gaurdant in pale, a bordure engrailed, or.
362. Monsr. Waut Pedwardyn.
   Gules, two lions passant in pale, or.
363. Monsr. John de Clyfton.
   Argent, a lion rampant within an orle of cinqfoils sable.
364. Monsr. Robt. Pedwardyn.
   Gules, two lions passant in pale or, a label of three points, argent.
365. Monsr. Willm. Bradsawe.
   Argent, two bendlets sable.
366. Monsr. John Dandeseye.
   Per pale or and argent, three bars nebulée, gules.
367. Monsr. Willm. de Acherton.
   Argent, two bendlets and a bordure sable.
368. Monsr. Willm. Wyngefeld.
   Gules, two wings conjoined in leure argent.
369. Mons. Ric. Abberbury.
   Or, a fess double embattled on the top sable, a label of three points, gules.

370. Monsr. John de Greseley.
   Vaire argent and gules.
371. Monsr. John Engayne.
   Azure, on a fess dancettée between six escalops argent, a mullet gules, pierced.
372. Monsr. Richard Constable.
   Quarterly gules and vaire, a bendlet or.
373. Monsr. Rauff Freschevill.
   Azure, a bend argent, charged in chief with a mullet gules, pierced, between six escalops of the second.
374. Monsr. Robt. Mawvesyn.
   Gules, three bendlets argent.
375. Mons. John Trellowe.
   Azure, a chevron between three escalops argent.
376. Monsr. Ric. Byron.
   Argent, three bendlets, gules.
377. Monsr. .... Peshale.
   Argent, a cross fleurée engrailed sable.
378. Monsr. John Trussell.
   Argent, a cross fleurée, gules.
379. Monsr. Thomas Lampelewe.
   Or, a cross fleurée sable.
380. Monsr. Moris de Berkele.
   Gules, a chevron ermine between six crosses patonce in chief and four in base, argent.
381. Monsr. Adam Peshale.
   Argent, a cross fleurée sable, on a quarter gules, a lion's head erased of the first, crowned or.

37

382. Monsr. James Berkele.
Gules, on a chevron between six crosses patonce in chief and four in base argent, a crescent azure.

383. Monsr. John Walsh.
Argent, a chevron between three fleurs de lis sable.

384. Monsr. John de Rodneye.
Or, three eagles displayed, two and one, gules.

385. Mons. Alnack de Aulaby.
Argent, a fess between six fleurs de lis sable.

386. Monsr. John Sayvill.
Argent, on a bend sable, three owls of the field.

387. Monsr. Robt. de Stafford.
Or, a chevron gules, surmounted by a bendlet azure.

388. Monsr. John Sayvill.
Argent, on a bend sable, three owls of the field; a label of three points, gules.

389. Monsr. John Nevyll.
Gules, semée of cross croslets fitchée, or, three leopards' heads of the last, jessant de lis, argent.

390. Monsr. Willm. Flamvill.
Argent, a manche azure.

391. Monsr. Henry Nevill.
Gules, semée of cross croslets fitchée, three leopard's heads jessant de lis or, on the first a crescent azure.

392. Monsr. Willm. Lambrun.
Argent, on a bend sable, cottised gules, three lions' heads erased of the field.

393. Monsr. Leonard Hakelytt.
   Argent, on a bend cottised sable, three mullets or, pierced azure.
394. Monsr. John de Rouche.
   Argent, on a bend cottised sable, three mullets of the field.
395. Monsr. Bryan Cornewaile.
   Ermine, a lion rampant gules, crowned or, a bordure engrailed, sable bezantée.
396. Monsr. John Blount.
   Azure, a saltire engrailed or.
397. Monsr. Thomas Blount.
   Quarterly argent and gules, on a bend sable, three eagles displayed, or.
398. Monsr. Thom. Blyg'feld.
   Argent, on a bend sable, three plates.
399. Monsr. Robt. Carbonel.
   Gules, a cross argent, a bordure engrailed or.
400. Monsr. Robt. Turk.
   Argent, on a bend azure between two lions rampant, gules, three bezants.
401. Monsr. Thom. Rersby.
   Gules, on a bend argent, three mullets sable, pierced.
402. Monsr. Waut. Cokeseye.
   Argent, on a bend azure, three cinqfoils or, pierced.
403. Monsr. John Hauberk.
   Argent, on a bend sable, three cinqfoils or, pierced.

404. Monsr. Willm. de Fulthorp.
Argent, a cross moline sable, charged with a crescent of the field.

405. Monsr. Robert Twyer.
Gules, a cross vaire.

406. Monsr. Robert Conyers.
Azure, a manche or, charged with an annulet sable.

407. Monsr. John Fastolf.
Quarterly or and azure, on a bend gules, three escalops argent.

408. Monsr. Alexander Walden.
Sable, two bars ermine, in chief three cinqfoils argent, pierced.

409. Monsr. de Etton.
Barry of twelve argent and gules, a label of three points azure, over all a canton sable, charged with a cross patonce, or.

410. Monsr. Willm. in le Bowes.
Ermine, three long bows erect, two and one gules.

411. Monsr. Richard Venables de ....
Argent, two bars azure, on a bend gules, three arrows of the field.

412. Monsr. John Boson.
Argent, three bird bolts erect, two and one, gules.

413. Monsr. Robert de Horsele.
Sable, three cinqfoils two and one, argent, pierced.

414. Monsr. John Thornebyry.
Argent, a chief or, surmounted by a lion rampant azure, over all two bendlets, gules.

415. Monsr. Robert de Zevelton.
Argent, two bars nebulée sable, a label of three points, gules.

416. Monsr. Edmonde de Frytheby.
Argent, three fleurs de lis, two and one, gules.

417. Monsr. Willm. de Spaygne.
Argent, a fess dancettée between three spaniels' heads erased sable.

418. Monsr. Adam de Rotherfield.
Gules, three fleurs de lis, two and one ermine.

419. Monsr. Thomas Gerberge.
Sable, a fess between two chevrons or.

420. Monsr. Alexander Goldingham.
Barry nebulée of six, ermine and gules.

421. Monsr. Thomas Cornerde.
Azure, a fess between two chevrons, or.

422. Monsr. John de Felton.
Gules, two lions passant in pale argent, within a double tressure, florée counter-florée or.

423. Monsr. Willm. Tendryng.
Azure, a fess between two chevrons, argent.

424. Monsr. Willm. de Wassington.
Argent, two bars gules, in chief three mullets of the last, pierced.

425. Monsr. John Skette.
Argent, a cross croslet sable.

426. Monsr. Philip la Vache.
Gules, three lions rampant, two and one argent, crowned or.
427. Monsr. Willm. Cog'sale.
Argent, a cross between four escalops, sable.
428. Monsr. Wauter Strykelande.
Sable, three escalops two and one, argent.
429. Monsr. John Reynes.
Chequy or and gules, a canton ermine.
430. Monsr. Thomas Tunstall.
Sable, three combs, two and one, argent.
431. Monsr. Willm. Mauleverere.
Gules, three greyhounds current in pale argent.
432. Monsr. Robert Kendale.
Argent, on a bend azure, three mullets or, pierced.
433. Monsr. Olyver Mauleverere.
Gules, three greyhounds current in pale argent, collared or.
434. Monsr. Henry Inglons.
Quarterly or and azure, in the first quarter a lion rampant sable.
435. Monsr. John Lakynghithe.
Argent, a chevron sable between three caps of the last turned up, gules.
436. Monsr. Robert Breton.
Azure, a bend between six mullets or, pierced.
437. Monsr. Payn Tiptoot.
Argent, a saltire engrailed, gules.

438. Monsr. Thomas le Brewes.
  Azure, semée of cross croslets, a lion rampant, or.
439. Monsr. Marmeduke Lumbney.
  Gules, on a fess between three popinjays argent, collared of the field, as many mullets of the last, pierced.
440. Monsr. John de Lodlowe.
  Or, a lion rampant, tail erect, sable.
441. Monsr. Thomas Notebeme.
  Gules, a fess nebulée ermine.
442. Monsr. Andrew Caundysh.
  Sable, three crosses botonnée fitchée or, two and one.
443. Monsr. Rauff Poley.
  Argent, on a bend gules, three crosses patée, or.
444. Monsr. Henry Coneway.
  Sable on a bend argent, cottised ermine, a rose gules between two annulets, or.
445. Monsr. Stephen Valans.
  Or, three pallets wavy gules, a bordure ermine.
446. Monsr. Richard Story.
  Argent, a lion rampant queue forchée purpure, charged on the shoulder with a cross patée, or.
447. Monsr. Nycoll Sarnesfeld.
  Azure, an eagle displayed, or.
448. Monsr. Wauter de la Leey.
  Argent, a fess between three crescents sable.
449. Monsr. Willm. Farendon.
  Gules, three cinqfoils, two and one, or.

450. Monsr. Nycoll Dagworthe.
    Ermine, on a fess gules, three torteaux.
451. Monsr. John Cheynn'.
    Chequy or and azure, a fess gules, frettée ermine.
452. Monsr. Willm. de Clivam.
    Argent, a fess gules, between three eagles displayed sable, armed of the second.
453. Monsr. Antoyn Mallory.
    Or, a lion rampant double queued, gules.
454. Monsr. John Golaffre.
    Barry nebulée of six, argent and gules, on a bend sable three bezants.
455. Monsr. Pirys Courtnay.
    Or, three torteaux, two and one; a label of three points, azure.
456. Monsr. Thomas West.
    Azure, three leopards' heads, jessant de lis or.
457. Monsr. Henry Grene.
    Argent, a cross engrailed gules.
458. Monsr. Willm. Chaworth.
    Azure, two chevronels, or.
459. Monsr. Gerrard Ufflet.
    Qrtly. 1 and 4, Or, a bend between six martlets, gules.
        2 and 3, Argent, on a fess azure, three fleurs de lis, or.
460. Monsr. John Sutton.
    Or, three chevronels, sable.
461. Monsr. John Copuldick.
    Argent, a chevron between three cross croslets, gules.

44

462. Monsr. Simond de la Pole.
    Azure, a fess between three tigers' faces, or.
463. Monsr. Thomas Oittrich.*
    Gules, on a cross patonce or, five mullets of six points of the field, pierced.
464. .... Voirnon.
    Qrtly. 1 and 4, Or, on a fess azure, three garbs of the field.
    2 and 3, Argent, a fret sable.
465. Monsr. Thomas Barr.
    Qrtly. 1 and 4, Gules, three bars componée argent and azure.
    2 and 3, Barry of six, or and azure, a bend, gules.
466. (No name.)
    Qrtly. 1 and 4, Argent, a cross voided, sable.†
    2 and 3, Argent, six annulets, three and three, gules.‡
467. S. Richard Redmane.
    Gules, three lozenge cushions ermine, two and one, tasseled or.
468. Monsr. Willm. de Hoo.
    Quarterly argent and sable.
469. Monsr. Thomas Maurwarde.
    Argent, a fess argent between three cinqfoils, or, pierced.

* Uchtred.   † Duckinfeld?   ‡ Plecy?

470. Monsr. John Elys.
   Or, on a cross sable, five escalops argent.
471. Monsr. Nicoll Goushull.
   Barry of six or and gules, a canton ermine.
472. Monsr. Nicoll son fits.
   Barry of six or and gules, a canton ermine, a label of three points, azure.
473. .... Plompton.
   Azure five fusils in fess or, each charged with an escalop, gules.
474. Monsr. Hipden.
   Ermine, five fusils in fess, gules.
475. (No name.*)
   Azure, five fusils in fess or, each charged with an escalop, gules; in the dexter chief a mullet argent.
476. Monsr. John de Dynham.
   Gules, four fusils in fess ermine.
477. Monsr. John Dauntr'.
   Sable, five fusils in fess argent.
478. Monsr. John Bosvill.
   Argent, five fusils in fess gules, in chief three martlets sable.
479. Monsr. Willm. Chetwynde.
   Azure, a chevron between three mullets, or.
480. Monsr. Thomas de Preston.
   Gules, five fusils in chief and three in base, argent.

* Evidently a cadet of No. 473.

481. Monsr. Willm. Chetwynde.
  Azure, a chevron between three mullets or, pierced.
482. Monsr. Robert Twyford.
  Argent, two bars sable, on a canton of the last, a cinqfoil or, pierced.
483. Monsr. Gefferey Warbirton.
  Argent, two chevronels gules, on a quarter of the last a mullet or.
484. Monsr. John Tryvett.
  Argent, a trivet within a bordure engrailed sable.
485. Monsr. Thomas Seint Cler.
  Gules, a fess between three lions' heads erased, or.
486. Monsr. John de Travers.
  Argent, a chevron between four butterflies sable.
487. Monsr. Gilbert Oulwenne.
  Argent, frettée gules, a chief azure.
488. Monsr. Bawdwy Pygot.
  Gules, three pickaxes, two and one argent.
489. Monsr. Robert Symeon.
  Gules, a fess or between three lions rampant argent.
490. Monsr. Randolff Pigot.
  Sable, three pickaxes, two and one argent.
491. Monsr. Ric. Grenacre.
  Sable, three covered cups, two and one argent.
492. Monsr. Gerrard Braybroke.
  Argent, seven mascles, gules, three, three and one; a label of three points, azure.

493. Monsr. Robt. Grenacre.
   Sable, an annulet between three covered cups, argent.
494. Monsr. John Beaumont.
   Barry of six, vaire and gules.
495. Monsr. Richard de Houghton,
   Sable, three bars argent, a label of three points, gules.
496. Monsr. Philip Daveye.
   Argent, on a chevron sable, between three mullets, gules, pierced, a crescent of the field.
497. Monsr. Robt. Hotot.
   Azure, a cross formée argent between four roses, or.
498. Monsr. John de la Mare.
   Gules, two lions passant gaurdant in pale argent.
499. Monsr. Roger de Beckham.
   Chequy or and sable, a fess ermine.
500. Monsr. John Giffard.
   Argent, ten torteaux, four, three, two and one.
501. Monsr. Roger Hillary.
   Sable, three fleurs de lis, between seven cross croslets fitchée, argent.
502. Monsr. Richard la Zouche. —
   Gules, ten bezants, four, three, two and one, a chief ermine.
503. Monsr. William Bonevill.
   Sable, six mullets, three, two and one, argent, pierced gules.
504. Monsr. John Talbott.
   Argent, three fleurs de lis, between seven cross croslets, fitchée gules.

48

505. Monsr. John de Walcote.
Argent, on a cross patonce azure, five fleurs de lis, or.
506. Monsr. Richard Acton.
Quarterly per fess indentée, argent and azure.
507. Monsr. Thomas Salman.
Argent, an eagle displayed sable, armed or, charged on the breast with a tiger's face of the last.
508. Monsr. Robert Fouleshurst.
Gules, frettée or, on a chief argent two mullets of six points sable, pierced.
509. Monsr. Thomas Grene.
Azure, three bucks statant, two and one, or.
510. Monsr. Roger Ledye.
Argent, a fess gules, between three eagles displayed, sable.
511. Monsr. Hugh le Hesy.
Or, on a fess sable, a lion passant gaurdant argent.
512. Monsr. John Basynges.
Gules, a fess argent, in chief one bar gemel, in base two bars gemels, of the last.
513. Monsr. Willm. Moton.
Argent, a cinqfoil azure, pierced.
514. Monsr. John Boyvill.
Gules, a fess or between three saltires, argent.
515. Monsr. John Dymoke.
Sable, two lions passant in pale argent, crowned or.
516. Monsr. John de Berkele.
Gules, a chevron between six cinqfoils in chief, and four in base, argent, pierced.

517. Monsr. Xpofer de Apr'sby.
    Sable, a cross argent, in the dexter chief a cinqfoil of the last, pierced.
518. Monsr. Thomas de Elande.
    Gules, two bars argent, between eight martlets of the last, three, two and three.
519. Monsr. Geffrey Brokeholes.
    Argent, a chevron between three badgers' heads erased, sable.
520. Monsr. Hugh de Northburgh.
    Gules, three roses argent, seeded or, between seven cross croslets fitchée of the second.
521. Monsr. Thomas de Burton.
    Sable, a chevron between three owls, argent, crowned or.
522. Monsr. Gilis d'Argentine.
    Gules, three covered cups, two and one, argent, garnished or.
523. Monsr. Thomas Gryffyn.
    Sable, a griffon segreant argent, armed or.
524. Monsr. John de Lancastre.
    Argent, a chevron between three eagles' legs erased, gules, a bordure engrailed sable.
525. Monsr. John de Coupelande.
    Argent, on a cross sable, a mullet of the field.
526. Monsr. Robert Moncastre.
    Barry of twelve, argent and gules, a bendlet azure.

527. Monsr. Willm. Seint Quyntoyne.
   Or, a chevron gules, a chief vaire.
528. Monsr. John de Peyton.
   Sable, a cross engrailed or, in the dexter chief a mullet argent.
529. Monsr. John Seint Quyntoyne.
   Or, on a chevron gules, a martlet of the field, a chief vaire.
530. Monsr. John de Byrmyngham.
   Per pale dancettée, argent and sable.
531. Monsr. Nicol Kyryell.
   Or, two chevronels and a quarter gules.
532. Monsr. Thomas de Broughton.
   Azure, a cross engrailed argent.
533. Monsr. John Plays.
   Per pale or and gules, a lion passant argent.
534. Monsr. Sampson de Strav'ley.
   Paly of six, argent and azure.
535. Monsr. Richard Vernon.
   Argent, frettée sable, a canton gules.
536. Monsr. Edmund de Beynham.
   Sable, three mallets, two and one, argent.
537. Monsr. John Br'wes.
   Argent, semée of cross croslets fitchée, a lion rampant, double queued, gules.
538. Monsr. Roger Tronyn.
   Sable, a saltire engrailed or.
539. Monsr. John le Roos.
   Ermine, three water budgets, two and one, gules.

540. Monsr. Thomas de Staw'ton.
    Argent, two chevronels sable, a bordure engrailed of the last.
541. Monsr. Yse ap Griffith.
    Gules, on a fess dancettée argent, between six lions rampant, or, three martlets sable.
542. Monsr. John Massy.
    Sable, a cross patonce or.
543. Monsr. Richard Chamberleyn.
    Gules, a chevron between three escalops, or.
544. Monsr. John de Cornewaile.
    Argent, three fusils in bend, between six cross croslets fitchée sable.
545. Monsr. Robert Bowne.
    Or, a cross azure.
546. Monsr. Roger Beauchamp.
    Gules, on a fess between six martlets or, a mullet sable, pierced.
547. Monsr. Robert de Morlee.
    Argent, a lion rampant sable, a label of three points, gules.
548. Monsr. Willm. Baude.
    Gules, three chevronels argent.
549. Monsr. Bernard Brocas.
    Sable, a lion rampant gaurdant or, a label of three points, gules.
550. Monsr. Rauff Basset de Weldon.
    Or, three pallets gules, on a bordure azure thirteen bezants.

551. Monsr. Edmond Noon.
   Or, a cross engrailed vert.
552. Monsr. John Molyns.
   Or, three pallets wavy, gules.
553. (Monsr. Jhon Ackland.)*
   Chequy argent and sable, a fess gules.
554. Monsr. John de Foxlee.
   Gules, two bars argent.
555. Monsr. Waut' Ursewycke.
   Argent, on a bend sable, three lozenges of the field, each charged with a saltire gules; in the sinister chief a crescent of the second.
556. Monsr. Piers de la Mare.
   Barry dancettée of six, or and gules.
557. Monsr. Thom. Wawton.
   Argent, a chevron sable, in the dexter chief an annulet of the last.
558. Monsr. Warren de Bassyngburn.
   Gyronny of twelve, or and azure.
559. (No name.)†
   Argent, on a chevron gules, three bezants, a bordure engrailed of the second.
560. Monsr. Bartram Monbocher.
   Argent, three pitchers, gules, two and one; on a bordure sable, twelve bezants.

* This in modern hand.   † Bromley?

661. Monsr. John Paynell de Knapcost.
Gules, a cross patonce, argent.
562. Monsr. John de Ypre.
Argent, a chevron between three bulls' heads caboshed, gules.
563. Monsr. Geffrey Withe.
Azure, three griffons passant in pale or, armed gules.
564. Monsr. Robt. Russell.
Gules, on a bend sable, fimbriated or, two mullets of the last, pierced of the field, and two swans argent; alternated.
565. Monsr. Thomas Morrewes.
Gules, on a bend argent, seven billets sable.
566. Monsr. Roger de Walsham.
Sable, a chevron argent, between three cinqfoils or, pierced.
567. Monsr. Nicoll Stukele.
Argent, on a fess sable, three mullets of the field.
568. Monsr. Willm. Bycovyleyn.
Argent, three crescents, two and one, gules.
569. Monsr. Willm. Smalberough.
Sable, a chevron between three bears' heads, couped or.
570. Monsr. Gerrard de Wythryngton.
Quarterly argent and gules, a bendlet sable.
571. Monsr. Roger de Tru'pington.
Azure, two trumpets in pile, or, between ten cross croslets of the last.

572. Monsr. Thomas Dale.
  Gules, a swan close, argent, membered sable.
573. Monsr. Thomas Colshill.
  Chequy argent and sable, [on the second cheque a crescent or,] a chief of the last.
574. Monsr. Willm. Dysney.
  Argent, three lions passant in pale, gules.
575. Monsr. John Seint Andrwe.
  Argent, a cross florée engrailed sable, on a bordure gules, eleven bezants.
576. Monsr. Robt. Barre.
  Gules, three bars embattled [on the top edge,] argent.
577. Monsr. Reynold Malignee.
  Ermine, on a fess gules, three pallets or.
578. Monsr. Leynard Hakelyut.
  Argent, on a bend cottised gules, three mullets or, pierced azure.
579. Monsr. John de Routh.
  Argent, on a bend cottised sable, three mullets of the field.
580. Monsr. John Walsh.
  Argent, a chevron between three fleurs de lis sable.
581. Monsr. John de Rodneye.
  Or, three eagles displayed, two and one, gules.
582. Monsr. Willm. Lamburn.
  Argent, on a bend sable, cottised gules, three lions' heads erased or.
583. Monsr. Alnach de Anlaby.
  Argent, a fess between six fleurs de lis sable.

584. .... Heron.
    Gules, three herons, two and one, argent, beaked and legged, or.
585. Monsr. Wauter Heron.
    Gules, three herons, two and one, argent, beaked and legged or, in chief a cross croslet of the last.
586. Monsr. Gerard Heron.
    Gules, three herons, two and one argent, beaked and legged or, in chief an annulet of the last.
587. Monsr. William Heron.
    Gules, a chevron engrailed between three herons, argent.
588. Monsr. Robert Herle.
    Gules, a chevron between three drakes, argent.
589. Monsr. John Heron.
    Gules, a chevron between three herons, argent.
590. Monsr. John de Burton.
    Argent, a bend wavy sable.
591. Monsr. Thomas Gissyng.
    Argent, on a bend azure three eagles displayed or, armed gules.
592. (No name.)*
    Sable, three hatchets erect argent, two and one.
593. Monsr. John Cokayn.
    Argent, three cocks, two and one, gules.†
594. Monsr. John Depden.
    Argent, on a chief azure, three lions rampant or.

* Denys?   † Vide Frontispiece.

56

595. (No name.*)
    Argent, three cocks sable, two and one, combs and
        wattles, gules.
596. Monsr. John de Irby.
    Argent, frettée sable, a quarter of the last.
597. Monsr. Thomas Bekerynge.
    Chequy argent and gules, on a chevron sable, three
        escalops of the first.
598. Monsr. Gilis Seint John.
    Gules, two bars argent, a quarter ermine.
599. .... Hercy.
    Gules, a chief argent.
600. Monsr. Richard Fytton.
    Argent, on a bend azure, three garbs or, in the sinister
        chief a crescent of the second.
601. Monsr. Robert Hovell.
    Sable, a cross or.

The end of the Arms.

At the extremity of the roll is written, in a hand apparently of the time of Elizabeth, " Ex dono Thome Moncke, Ar."

* Pomfret?

INDEX.

ABBERBURY, Rich. Nos. 197, 369.
Acherton, Will. de, 367.
Ackland, John, 553.
Acton, Richard, 506.
Anlaby, Alnach de, 385, 583.
Annesley, John de, 182.
Ap Griffith, Yse, 541.
Appelby, Edmond, 180.
Aprs'by, Christofer de, 517.
Argentine, Giles de, 522.
Arundel, de Conte d', 52.
Astley, 92.
—— Thos. de, 235.
—— de Morton, Thos. de, 237.
Attewode, John, 167.
Awdely, James d', 20.
Awawton, Will. 211.
Aylesbury, John de, 254.
——— Thomas, 255.

Badlismere, Le Sr. de, 43.
Bagot, John, 281.
—— Willm. 267.
Bardolf, Le Sr. le, 56.
Barr, Thomas, 465.
Barre, Robert, 567.
—— Willm. 361.
Basset, John, 178.
—— de Weldon, Ralph, 550.
Bassingburn, Warren de, 558.
Basynges, John, 512.
Baude, Willm. 548.

Beauchamp, John, 9.
————— Roger, 546.
————— Willm. 83.
————— de Somerset, Le Sr. le, 72.
————— Conte de Warwick, 2, 35.
Beaufort, John, 134.
Beaumont, John, 494.
————— Le Sr. le, 46.
Beekham, Roger, 499.
Bekerynge, Thomas, 597.
Bellers, James, 168.
Beresforde, Bawdwyn, 131.
Berkeley, James, 382.
———— John de, 516.
———— Moris de, 380.
———— Le Sr. le, 57.
Beulee, Ric. de, 296.
Beynham, Edmond de, 536.
Birlande, Willm. 358.
Blount, John, 396.
—— Thomas, 397.
—— Walter, 188.
Blygfeld, Thomas, 398.
Bolesby, Will. de. 334.
Bonatlem, John, 313.
Bonevill, Willm. 503.
Boson, John, 412.
Bosvill, John, 478.
Boteler, Edward, 288.
—— John, 287, 289.
Botrewes, Will. 89.
Botourt, Le Sr. le, 76.

Bouch, Le Capit. de, 3.
Boughton, Peris de, 329.
Bourchier, Barthol. 8, 129.
———— Le Sr. le, 73.
Bowes, Will. in le, 410.
Bowne, Robert, 545.
Boys, Roger le, 225.
Boynton, Thom. de, 339.
Boyvill, John, 514.
Bradsawe, Willm. 365.
Brasbrige, Ralph, 299.
Braybroke, Gerard de, 143, 492.
Brewes, John, 537.
———— Thomas le, 438.
Britchebury, Avery, 279.
Brocas, Bernard, 162, 549.
Brokeholes, Geffrey, 519.
Bromley, 559.
Broughton, Thos. de, 532.
Browe, Hugh de, 283,
Bryan, Guy de, 90.
———— Willm. le, 128.
Bulmer, Ralph, 105.
Bur, Willm. 261.
Burdet, John, 291.
Burghersh, 8.
Burnel, Le Sr. le, 70.
Burton, John de, 590.
———— Thomas de, 521.
Burwash, 8.
Bussy, John, 154.
Bycovyleyn, Willm. 568.
Byngham, Rich. de, 317.
Byllynge, Nicol, 294.
Byrmingham, John de, 530.
Byron, Richard, 376.
Byrton, John de, 222.

Calveley, Hugh de, 84, 243.
———— John de, 241.
Camoys, Le Sr. le, 77.
Carbonel, Robert, 399.
Carew, Pers de, 277.
Caundysh, Andrew, 442.
Chamberlain, Richd. 543.

Chandos, John, 19.
———— Walter, 236.
Charleton, Le Sr. de, 61.
Chaworth, Willm. 458.
Chetwynde, Willm. 479, 481.
Cheyne, Ralph, 302,
———— Thomas, 298.
Cheynn, John, 451.
Clarendon, Roger de, 133.
Clavering, John, 246.
———— Robert, 244.
Clifford, Lewis de, 115.
———— Robert de, 126.
———— Le Sr. de, 48.
Clifton, John de, 363.
———— Nicol de, 249.
———— Robert de, 247.
Clinton, John de, 101.
———— Thomas de, 190.
Clivam, Willm. de, 452.
Cobham, Thos. de, 260.
———— Raynold de, 93.
———— Le Sr. de, 65.
Cogsale, Willm. 427.
Cokayne, John, 593.
Cokeseye, Walter, 402.
Colpeper, Thos. 118.
Colshill, Thos. 573.
Colvil, 319.
Colvyle, John, 165, 252.
Constable, Richard, 372.
Conway, Henry, 444.
Conyers, Robert, 406.
Copuldick, John, 461.
Corbet, Robert, 223, 224.
Cornerde, Thos. 421.
Cornwall, Bryan, 395.
Cornewaile, John de, 544.
Cosynton, Willm. de, 119.
Coupelande, John de, 525.
Courtenay, Hugh, 11.
———— Philip, 107.
———— Pirys, 455.
———— Conte de Devonshire, 38.
Craddock, Rich. 357.

Criol, Nicol, 531.
Cromwell, Sr. de Tateshall, Ralph, 110.
Curson, Roger, 305.

Dabrichecourt, John de, 322.
——————— Nicol, 320.
——————— Sancett, 23.
Dacre, Le Sr. de 75.
Dagworthe, Nycoll, 450.
Dale, Thomas, 572.
Dandeseye, John, 366.
Darcy, Le Sr. 54.
Daveye, Philip, 496.
Dauntrey, John, 477.
Deggar Sees. Vide Sees.
De la Bere, Rynard, 215.
De la Mare, John, 498.
——————— Piers, 556.
De la Pole, Michael, 130.
——————— Simond, 482.
De le Pole, John, 345.
Denys, 502.
Depden, John, 594.
Derby, Le Conte de, 29.
Derwentwater, John, 228.
Devereux, John, 98, 251.
Devonshyre, Le Conte de, 38.
Deyncourt, John, 156.
——————— Le Sr. le, 74.
Dodyngsel, John, 292.
Dukinfeld, 466.
Dutton, Lawrence de, 284.
Dyks, Willm. de, 266.
Dymoke, John 515.
Dynham, John de, 476.
Dysney, Willm. 574.

Eam, Henry, 22.
Edward III, King, 1.
Elande, Thos. de, 518.
Elys, John, 470.
Engayne, John, 371.
Ermyne, Willm. de, 331.
Eruington, Thom. de, 351.
Erpingham, Thomas, 207.
Etton, de, 409.

Exeter, Duke of, 36.
Everingham, Laurens, 285.
——————— Reynold de, 87.
Everwyke, Le Duc de, 27.
Eynesford, John de, 187, 189.

Fallesle, John de, 147.
Farendou, Willm. 449.
Fastolf, John, 407.
Fauconberg, Roger, 176.
——————— Le Sr. le, 78.
Felbrig, George, 174.
——————— Simond, 173.
Felton, John de, 422.
Fenwick, John, 183.
Ferrers, Robert, 153.
——————— Le Sr. de, 94.
——————— de Groby, Le Sr. de, 67.
Fitz Henry, Thomas, 201.
Fitz Hugh, Edmund, 286.
——————— Henry, 138.
Fitz John, Randolph, 336.
Fitz Nicol, Thomas, 256.
Fitz Symond, Richard, 14.
——————— Thos. 123.
Fitz Walter, Le Sr. 45.
Fitz Waryu, 137, 141.
Fitz William, Willm. 245.
Flamvill, Willm. 390.
Flemyng, Thomas, 346.
Foljamb, Godfrey, 307.
Fogge, Thomas, 179.
Fouleshurst, Robt. 508.
Foxlee, John de, 554.
Franceis, Adam, 164.
Fraunceys, Robert, 311.
Freschevil, Ralph, 373.
Frevill, Baudewyn, 114.
Frytheby, Edmund de, 416.
Fulthorp, Will. de, 404.
Fytton, Richard, 600.

Gerberge, Thos. 419.
Gery, John, 221.
Giffard, John, 500.
Gissing, Thomas, 591.

Gloucester, Le Duc de, 28.
Goderiche, Willm. 359.
Gollafre, John, 454.
Goldesborow, Rich. de, 272.
Goldingham, Alex. 420.
Gournay, Mays, 104.
Goushull, Nicoll, 471, 472.
Gray, Thomas, 116.
Grenacre, Rich. 491.
——— Robt. 493.
Grene, Henry, 457.
——— Thomas, 509.
Greseley, John de, 370.
Grey, John, 13.
——- Rich. 344.
——- de Connor, Le Sr. 44.
——- de Rotherfield, Le Sr. 64.
——- de Ruffyn, Le Sr. 50.
——— de Wilton, Henry, 109.
Greystock, Le Baron de, 88.
Gryffin, Thomas, 523.
Gryffith, Yse ap, 541.
Grymesby, John de, 340.
Grymston, Gerrard de, 301.
Hakelyut, Leonard, 393, 578.
Hakenbeche, Reynald, 209.

Hales, Steven de, 314.
Harcourt, Thomas, 132.
Haryngton, Nicol, 194.
——————— Le Sr. de, 68.
Hasteley de Morton, Thos. 237.
Hastings, Ralph, 96.
Hauberk, John, 403.
Hawarde, John, 200.
Hawkewode, John, 152.
Hawley, Thomas, 332.
Hemnale, Thos. 300.
Hengrave, Edmond, 335.
Hercy, 599.
Herle, Robert, 588.
Heron, 584.
——— Gerard, 586.
——— John, 589.
——— Walter, 585.
——— William, 587.

Herpyngham, Thos. de, 205.
Hesy, Hugh le, 511.
Hetou, Henry de, 169.
Hillary, Roger, 501.
Hilton, Le Baron de, 97.
Hipden, 474.
Hodelston, John, 191.
Holgom, John de, 349.
Holland, John de, 160.
——— Otes, 21.
——— Thomas, 12.
——— et Lovel, Le Sr. d
——— Conte de Kent, 34
——————— Hunting·
——— Duke de Exeter,
Hoo, Willm. de, 468.
Horsele, Robt. de, 413.
Hotot, Robt. 497.
Hovell, Robt. 601.
Houghton, Rich. de, 140, 4!
Howard, v. Hawarde.
Huntingdon, Le Conte de,·

Ingesthorp, John de, 304.
Inglons, Henry, 434.
Ipre, John de, 562.
——— Ralph de, 315.
Irby, John de, 596.

Kendale, Robert, 432.
Kent, Le Conte de, 34.
Kentwode, John, 196.
Knolles, Robert, 102.
Kydeley, Thos. 338.
Kyrkeby, Rich. de, 227.
Kyryell, Nicol, 531.

Lakynghithe, John, 435.
Lamburu, Willm. 392, 582.
Lampelewe, Thos. 379.
Lancaster, John de, 524.
——— William de, 226.
——— John Duc de, 26.
Langeton, Christoph. de, 265.
Laton, Robt. de, 233.
——— Willm. de, 356.

INDEX. 61

Latymer, Thomas, 145.
La Warre, Le Sr. 53.
Ledye, Roger, 510.
Leey, Walter de la, 448.
Leybourne, Thos. 354.
Leyke, Andrew de, 238.
—— John de, 239.
—— Robt. de, 240.
Lilbourne, John, 264.
Lisle, John de, 7.
——- Willm. de, 203.
——- Le Sr. de le, 59.
Littlebury, John, 360.
Lodlowe, John de, 440.
Longeford, Nich. de, 220.
Lorryng, Neel, 18.
Lotrel, Andrew, 248.
Lovel et Holland, Le Sr. de, 62.
Lucy, Geoffrey, 232.
——- Reynold, 234.
——- Conte de Northumberland. Sr. de, 39.
Ludlow, John de, 440.
Lumley, Marmaduke, 409.
——— Ralph, 100.
Lutrel, Andrew, 248.
—— Hugh, 214.

Malignee, Reynold, 577.
Mallory, Antoyn, 453.
Manners, John, 204.
Marche, Le Conte de la, 6, 31.
Marchyngton, Thos. 280.
Mardak, John, 192.
Marischall, Le Conte, 33.
Marny, Robert, 161.
—— Willm. 163.
Massy, John, 542.
Mauleverere, Oliver, 433.
——————— Willm. 431.
Maurwarde, Thomas, 469.
Mawvesyn, Robt. 374.
Melton, Willm. de, 268.
Metham, Thos. de, 121.
Missenden, Edmond de, 347.
Mohun, 10.
Moigne, Willm. 185.

Molyns, John, 552.
Monboucher, Bertram, 560.
Moncastre, Robert, 526.
Mongomery, Nicol, 250.
Montacute, John, 91.
————— Conte de Salisbury, 5, 37.
Morley, Robt. de, 547.
—— Le Sr. de, 60.
Morrewes, Thomas, 565.
Moton, Willm. 513.
Moubray, Thos. 79.
————— Le Conte Maryschall, Sr. de, 33.
Mounceneye, John, 216.
————— Robt. 217.
Mounford, Thos. 177.
Musgrave, Thos. 181.

Nevill, Alexand. 333.
——— Henry, 391.
——— John, 389.
——— Robert, 139.
——— Le Sr. de, 47.
——— Thomas, 135.
——— William, 108.
Noon, Edmund, 551.
Norlonde, Rich. 111.
Northburgh, Hugh de, 520.
Northumberland, Le Conte de, 39.
Notebeme, Thomas, 441.

Oittrich, Thos. 463.
Ogle, Robert, 151.
Oker, Philip de, 282.
Oulwenne, Gilbert, 487.
Oxford, Le Conte de, 41.

Papenham, Laurence de, 348.
Pappeworth, Willm. de, 230.
Passele, Robt. de, 259.
Paveley, Walter, 24.
Paynell, John, 341.
——— de Knapcost, John, 561.
Pedwardyn, Robt. 364.
——— Walter, 362.
Peeche, John, 166.

Pekbrugge, John, 312.
Percy, Henry, 81.
——— Ralph, 124.
——— Thomas, 80.
——— Conte de Northumberland, 39.
Peshale, 377.
——— Adam, 381.
Peyton, John de, 528.
Pickworth, Robert, 310.
——— Thomas, 308.
Pickering, James le, 171.
——— Robert, 170.
Pierpoint, Edmond, 355.
Pigot, Bawdwy, 488.
——— Randolph, 490.
Plays, John, 533.
Plecy, 466.
Plompton, 473, 475.
Poinings, Le Sr. le, 66.
Pole, John de le, 345.
——— Michael de la, 130.
——— Symond ———, 462.
Poley, Ralph, 443.
Pomeray, John, 175.
Pomfret, 595.
Predias, John, 212.
Preston, Thos. de, 480.
Ramston, Thos. de, 213.
Redmayne, Mays, 112.
——— Thomas, 467.
Rersby, Thos. 401.
Reynes, John, 429.
——— Thos. 201.
Richard II. King, 25.
Rocheford, John, 158.
——— Rauff. 159.
Rodney, John de, 384, 581.
Rokeby, Thos. de, 295.
Rokeley, Robt. de, 324.
Roos, James le, 253.
——— John le, 539.
——— Robt. le, 263.
——— Thomas le, 262.
——— William le, 127.
——— et de Badlesmere, Le Sr. le, 43.

Rotherfield, Adam de, 418.
Rouche, John de, 394.
Routh, John de, 579.
Russell, Robt. 564.
Rutland, Le Conte, 30.
Rydford, Henry de, 330.
Rylleston, Willm. de, 342.

Sackville, Thos. 257, 258.
St. Andrew, John, 575.
St. Amand, Le Sr. de, 58.
St. Cler, Thos. 485.
St. George, Bawdwyn, 172.
St. John, Edw. 337.
——— Giles, 598.
——— Le Sr. le, 69.
St. Leger, Ralph, 326.
——— Renold, 328.
St. Quintin, John, 529.
——— William, 527.
Salisbury, Le Conte de, 5, 37.
Salman, Thos. 507.
Salvayne, Gerard, 199.
Saly, Willm. 297.
Staveley, Sampson de, 534.
Sarnesfeld, Nycoll, 447.
Savage, Arnold, 353.
Saville, John, 386, 388.
Scales, Le Sr. le, 55.
Scargil, Willm. 306.
Scrope, 148.
——— Henry le, 82, 146.
——— John le, 144.
——— Richard le, 99.
——— Steven le, 150.
——— Thomas le, 136.
——— William le, 142.
Sees, Diggory, 95.
Seyton, John de, 218.
Shelton, Ralph de, 323, 325.
Shirley, Hugh de, 270.
Skette, John, 425.
Sleght, Robt. 274.
Smalborough, Willm. 569.
Soardeby, John, 293.

Southworth, Thos. 316.
Spaygne, Willm. de, 417.
Spencer, Hugh le, 125.
———— Philip, 86.
———— Le Sr. le, 42.
Stafford, Le Conte de, 4, 40.
———— Edmund de, 103.
———— Humphry de, 184.
———— Nicol de, 186.
———— Robert de, 387.
———— Thomas de, 4.
Stapleton, Bryan de, 113.
———— Miles de, 15, 120.
Staunton, Thos. de, 540.
Story, Richard, 446.
Strange, John le, 350, 352,
———— Le Sr. le, 51.
Strickland, Walter, 428
Strothere, Thos. de, 202.
Stukeley, Nicoll, 567.
Sutton, John, 460
Swallow, Willm. 309.
Swillington, Robt. de, 157.
Swinburne, Robt. 208.
———— Thos. 210.
———— Willm. 343.
Symeon, Robert, 489.

Talbot, Gilbert, 198.
———— John, 504.
———— Richard, 71.
———— Thomas, 122.
Taylboys, Walter, 327.
Tempist, Rich. 219.
Tendring Willm. 423.
Thornbury, John, 414.
Thorpe, Edmund de, 303.
———— John de, 229.
Tiptoft, Payne, 437.
Tiringham, John de, 242.
Touchet, 290.
Travers, John de, 486.
Trayly, John, 149.
Trellowe, John, 375.
Tronyn, Roger, 538.

Trumpington, Roger de, 571.
Trussell, Avery, 195.
———— John, 378.
Tryvett John, 484.
Tunstall, Thos. 430.
Turk, Robt. 400.
Twyer, Robt. 405.
Twyford, Robt. 482.

Vache, Philip la, 426.
Valans, Stephen, 445.
Vavasor, Willm. de, 231.
Venables, Richd. de, 411.
Verdon, John, 193.
Vere, Aubrey le, 106.
———— Conte de Oxinford, 41.
Vernon, 464.
———— Richard, 535.

Uchtred, 463.
Ufflete, Gerrard, 459.
Ulster, Le Conte de, 31.
Umfraville, Thos. 278.
Urswick, Robt. de, 275.
———— Walter, 555.

Walcote, John de, 505.
Waldegrave, Richd. 155.
Walden, Alexr. 408.
Wale, Thos. 16.
Walsh, John, 383, 580.
———— Thomas, 276.
Walsham, Roger de, 566.
Warburton, Geoffrey, 483.
Warde, John, 273.
Warre, Le Sr. la, 53.
Warren, Le Conte de, 32.
Warwick, Le Conte de, 2, 35.
Wassington, Willm. de, 424.
Wawton, Willm. a, 211.
———— Thomas a, 557.
Welles, Le Sr. de, 63.
Wennesley, Thos. de, 271.
West, Thomsa, 456.
Whitneye, Robt. de, 321.

Willoughby, Edmund, 318.
—————— Le Sr. de, 52.
Wilton, John de, 269.
Wingfield, Willm. 368.
Withe, Geoffrey, 563.
Witherington, Gerrard de, 570.
Wriothesley, Hugh de, 17.

York, Le Duc de, 27.
Ypre, John de, 562,
—————— Ralph de, 315.

Zevelton, Robt. de, 415.
Zouche, Hugh la, 85.
—————— Richard la, 502.
—————— Le Sr. la, 49.

FINIS

Autograph Manuscripts, Missals,
PRINTS,
AND LITERARY MISCELLANIES,
11, OXFORD STREET, (CORNER OF GEORGE STREET,)
MANCHESTER,

Begs to draw the attention of Virtuosi, Collectors, and the Public, to his remarkably varied Stock, consisting of

BOOKS.—A most extensive assemblage of all Ages, from the Invention of Printing to the Present Time, in all Classes of Literature, and in all Languages; the whole warranted perfect, unless otherwise expressed.

AUTOGRAPHS.—The largest Collection extant, including Specimens of the Writing of Celebrated Individuals of all Ages and Countries; the whole guaranteed genuine, without positively described as doubtful.

PORTRAITS.—A Collection varying from Ten to Twenty Thousand, adapted for Illustration, kept for the most part Alphabetically Arranged; also larger Prints, suited for Framing or the Folio.

TOPOGRAPHICAL PRINTS, extending over the whole Counties, but more particularly relating to those Counties local to his place of business, respecting which his Collections are of remarkable extent.

PRINTS suited for Framing or the Folio.—A Choice Selection, both English and Foreign, Ancient and Modern, more extensive than is usually seen.

SCRAP PRINTS, adapted for Scrap Books, Albums, Illustration, Screens, &c. &c.—An endless variety.

LITERARY MISCELLANIES, comprising everything that can be brought under such a denomination, both Curious and Useful.

STATIONERY of all kinds, from the best Makers.—Cream Laid Note Paper, 2s. 9d., 3s. 6d., and 5s. 6d. per Ream; Adhesive Envelopes to match, 6d., 8d., 1s., and 1s. 6d. per 100.

J. G. BELL is preparing for Publication by Subscription, the following Valuable Works:—

ST. GEORGE'S Heraldic Visitation of the County of Northumberland in 1615. Folio, *many illustrations*, 21s.; or Large Paper, £2 2s.; or Large Paper, with the Arms Emblazoned, £5 5s.

Genealogical and Biographical History of the County of Devon, *with illustrations*, compiled from Manuscripts in the British Museum, and other Authentic Sources, by C. J. TUCKER, Esq.

Descriptive and Critical Catalogue of Works Illustrated by THOMAS and JOHN BEWICK, Wood Engravers. 2nd Edition, with many Additions, and suitable Illustrations, printed to rank with Bewick's Principal Works, 8vo. 7s. 6d.; royal 8vo., 10s. 6d.; and imperial 8vo. 14s.

11, OXFORD STREET, MANCHESTER.

CATALOGUE OF BOOKS, PRINTS, AUTOGRAPHS, and LITERARY MISCELLANIES, just Published, may be had gratis, or sent Post-free for 4 Stamps.

ANGLING. A Paper on the Pleasure and Utility of Angling, by William Andrew Mitchell, 12mo woodcut by Bewick, sewed, 1s. 1824

AUTOGRAPHS. Selections from an Autograph Collection, comprising Letters of Individuals eminent in History and Literature, 8vo. *only 50 copies privately printed*, 2s. 1852

BERKSHIRE. A Glossary of Provincial Words used in Berkshire, post 8vo. sewed, 1s., sells for 1s. 6d. 1825

BOSVILLE FAMILY. Some Account of Maidstone in Kent, *with facsimile of an Ancient Sketch of the Market Place there*, to which are added Genealogical Tables of the Bosville Family, by J. H. Baverstock, F.S.A., their Descendant, imp. 8vo. *only one hundred copies printed for sale*, 4s. 6d. *Nicholls and Son*, 1832

BROUGHAM. Portrait of Henry Brougham, Lord Brougham and Vaux, drawn on Stone by Templeton, after a Painting by Ross, *India proofs*, 1s.; pub. 12s. 1840

CHESHIRE. An Attempt at a Glossary of some Words used in Cheshire, by Roger Wilbraham, Esq., F.R.S., F.S.A., 12mo. bds. 2s. 6d., pub. 6s. 1826

CIVIL WARS. The Taking of Gateshead Hill and Blocking of Newcastle, also the Defeat of the Oxford Forces near Abingdon, and Particulars of the Victory at Burton, reprinted from the edition of 1644, post 8vo. sewed, 1s. 1851

CIVIL WARS. Great Newes from Newcastle, giving an Account of the Scots Army before that Towne, from the 27th of August to the 4th of September, 1640, post 8vo. sewed, *rare*, 1s. 1851

COMMISSION SPECIALLY DIRECTED TO THE EARL OF HUNTINGDON, Her Majesty's Lieutenant in the North Parts, and others, for the Care and Defence of the Borders of England for and against Scotland, February 23, A.D. 1592, Eliz. 35, post 8vo. 1s. 1851

COSTUME. Specimens of Ecclesiastical Costume, from the Earliest Period to the 16th Century, selected from Sculptures, Paintings, and Brasses remaining in this Kingdom, by John Carter, F.S.A., 8vo. 7 *plates*, bds. 3s. 6d., pub. at 10s. 6d. 1817

COSTUMES OF THE MONASTIC ORDERS, 21 *plates*, from Stevens' edition of Dugdale's Monasticon, the Descriptions from Fosbrooke, 4to. 4s., pub. 8s.

CUMBERLAND. Glossary of Provincial Words used in the County of Cumberland, post 8vo. sewed, 1s. 6d. 1851

DIALECT. The Howdy and the Upgetting, Two Tales of 60 Years sin Seyne, as related by the late Thomas Bewick, in the Tyneside Dialect, post 8vo. *portrait, &c.* 2s. 6d. 1850

DORSET. A Glossary of Provincial Words used in the County of Dorset, post 8vo. sewed, 1s. 1851

DURHAM. General View of the Agriculture of the County of Durham, with Observations on the Means of its Improvement, by John Bailey, 8vo. *coloured map, plates, and woodcuts, the latter by Bewick*, bds. 2s., pub. 10s. 6d. 1810

EDWARD GLENHAM. The honourable Actions of the most Famous and Valiant Englishman, Edward Glenham, that he obtained against the Spaniards, 1581, 8vo. *private reprint, very scarce*, 2s.

ESSEX. Glossary of Provincial Words used in the County of Essex, post 8vo. sewed, 1s. 6d. 1851

FALSE PROPHETS DISCOVERED, being a true Story of the Lives and Deaths of two Weavers of Colchester, small 4to. *privately printed*, 2s. 1844

FACSIMILE OF A LETTER FROM THOMAS BEWICK, the Celebrated Wood Engraver, respecting his History of Quadrupeds, 1s.

FERGUSON. The Poetical Works of Robert Ferguson, with his Life, 2 vols. foolscap 8vo. *woodcuts by Thomas Bewick*, cloth, 7s. 6d, pub. at 12s. *Alnwick*.

GEOLOGY. The Certainties of Geology, by William Sydney Gibson, Esq., F.G.S., F.A.S., &c. &c., 8vo. cloth, 3s., pub. 10s. 6d. 1840

GLOSSARY OF TERMS USED IN THE COAL TRADE OF NORTHUMBERLAND AND DURHAM, second edition, 8vo. sewed, 2s. 1851

GLOUCESTERSHIRE. Glossary of Provincial Words used in Gloucestershire, with Proverbs current in that County, post 8vo. sewed, 1s. 6d. 1851

GOLDSMITH. The Poetical Works of Oliver Goldsmith, M.B., with the Life of the Author, 12mo. *woodcuts by T. Bewick*, bds. 3s., pub. 6s. 1809

GROSE'S ANTIQUITIES OF ENGLAND AND WALES, 4to. divided into Counties, with title-pages to each, thereby, as far as practicable, making each County a distinct work.

Bedfordsh. 7 *plates*, 1s. 6d. (letter-press imperfect)
Berksh. 7 *plates*, 1s. 9d.
Buckinghamsh. 5 *plates*, 1s (letter-press imperfect)
Cambridgesh. 5 *plates*, 1s. 3d.
Cornwall, 24 *plates*, 6s.
Dorsetsh., 12 *plates*, 3s.
Gloucestersh., 10 *plates*, 2s. 6d.
Hampsh. 42 *plates*, 10s.
Herefordsh. 8 *plates*, 2s.
Hettfordsh. 9 *plates*, 2s. 3d.
Kent, 56 *plates*, 14s.
Leicestersh. 5 *plates*, 1s. (letter-press imperfect)
Middlesex, 11 *plates*, 2s. 6d. (letter-press imperfect)
Monmouthsh. 12 *plates*, 2s.
Nottinghamsh. 4 *plates*, 1s.
Staffordsh. 5 *plates*, 1s. 3d.
Surrey, 21 *plates*, 5s. 3d.
Warwicksh. 10 *plates*, 2s. 6d.
Westmoreland, 4 *plates*, 1s.
Wiltsh. 8 *plates*, 2s.
Worcestersh. 7 *plates*, 1s. 9d.
Yorksh. 55 *plates*, 13s. 6d.
Isle of Lundi, 3 *plates*, 9d.
Anglesea, 8 *plates*, 2s.
Brecknocksh. 2 *plates*, 6d.
Carmarthensh. 4 *plates*, 1s.
Carnarvonsh. 12 *plates*, 3s.
Cardigansh. 3 *plates*, 9d.
Denbighsh. 3 *plates*, 9d.
Flintsh. 11 *plates*, 2s. 9d.
Glamorgansh. 20 *plates*, 5s.
Montgomerysh. 6 *plates*, 1s. 6d.
Pembrokesh. 11 *plates*, 2s. 9d.

HAMMERSMITH. The History and Antiquities of the Parish of Hammersmith, interspersed with Biographical Notices of Illustrious Personages, &c., by Thomas Faulkner, 8vo. *portraits and plates*, cloth, 6s., pub. £1 1s. 1839

HERALDIC VISITATION. The Visitation of ye County Palatyne of Durham, in the Yeare of Our Lorde God, 1575, by William Flower, edited by Nicholas John Philipson, Esq., folio, *copiously illustrated with wood engravings of arms, finely engraved title, &c.* bds. 12s. 6d., pub. at £2 2s. Only 100 copies of this beautiful work were printed. *Newcastle*, 1820
—— The same, on *large paper, with India proof of the title*, royal folio, bds. 20s., pub. £3 3s. *Ib.*
—— ST. GEORGE'S HERALDIC VISITATION OF WESTMORELAND in 1615; reduced to Narrative Form from the Original MSS., post 8vo. cloth, 4s.; or large paper, 4to. scarce, 8s. 1853

HERALDRY. Description of the Arms of the Counties, Chief Towns, and Boroughs in England and Wales, with their Origin, and Directions how to correctly Emblazon the same, also a Glossary of Heraldic Terms, 18mo. sewed, 1s. 1848
—— WYRLEY'S True Use of Arms, reprinted from the Original Edition, with Preface, post 8vo. *only 75 copies printed*, plates, cloth, 4s. 6d. 1853
—— The same, *on large paper*, 4to. cloth, *only 20 copies printed*, 9s.
—— Facsimile from W. Wyrley's Copy in 1592, of Fowler and Clover's Visitation of Derbyshire made in 1569, 2 large sheets, *numerous arms, private lithograph, very rare*, 4s.
—— PLAYFAIR'S Short Inquiry into the Nature of Heraldry, from his large Work on Genealogy, royal 4to. *plates*, 2s.

LONDON PAGEANTS. Accounts of 55 Royal Processions and Entertainments in the City of London, with an Account of the Preparations for the Entertainment of King William and Queen Adelaide, in 1831, also a Biographical List of Lord Mayors' Pageants, 8vo. *plate and woodcuts*, 1s. 6d., pub. at 2s. 6d. *Nichols*, 1837

MECHANICS. Essays on Practical Mechanics, by Thomas Fenwick, Colliery Viewer, 8vo. *plates*, 2s., pub. at 12s. 1822

MEMOIRS OF MARMADUKE TUNSTALL, ESQ., AND GEORGE ALLAN, ESQ., together with Notices of the Works of Thomas Bewick, by G. T. Fox, F.L.S., 8vo. *portrait, pedigree, and plate of arms*, 2s. 1827

MEMORIALS OF THE REBELLION IN THE NORTH OF ENGLAND, of 1569, chiefly compiled from the Bowes Papers at Streatlam Castle, 8vo. *illustrated with portraits, facsimiles, and woodcuts*, cloth, *very few printed*, 10s., pub. at £1 11s. 6d. 1840

MONASTIC LITERATURE. Remarks on the Mediæval Writers of English History, intended as a Popular Sketch of the Advantages and Pleasures derivable from Monastic Literature, by William Sydney Gibson, Esq., F.S.A., &c. &c., 8vo. 1s. 6d., pub. at 2s. 6d. *Pickering*, 1848

MURRAY'S (LINDLEY) ENGLISH READER, designed to Assist Young Persons to Read with Propriety and Effect, 12mo. bound, 2s., pub. at 3s. 6d. 1842
—— ENGLISH EXERCISES, adapted to Murray's English Grammar, 12mo. bound, 1s. 6d., pub. at 2s. 1843
—— ENGLISH GRAMMAR, adapted to the different Classes of Learners, with an Appendix, 8vo. roan, 2s., pub. at 3s. 6d. 1834

NICHOLL'S HISTORICAL NOTICES OF FONTHILL ABBEY, Wiltshire, 4to., 11 *fine plates and woodcuts*, bds., 5s., pub. at 15s. 1836

Critical, and Poetical, 12mo. bds. 1s. 6d., pub. at 6s. 1824
PORTRAIT OF THOMAS BEWICK, Engraved by Burnett, after a Picture by Ramsay, 1s.; or
India proof, 1s. 6d.
☞ A new impression taken from the original plate. This is the best likeness of Bewick, and was originally published at 21s.
PORTRAIT OF THE REV. FRANCIS CROSSMAN, Minister of Holland Episcopal Chapel, Brixton, engraved by Barnard, after a Picture by Salter, 1s. 6d., pub. at 21s. 1838
PRESBYTERIANISM. Historical Memorials of Presbyterianism in Newcastle-upon-Tyne, by an Episcopalian, post 8vo. cloth, 1s. 6d., pub. at 3s. 6d. 1847
RICHBOROUGH. A little Dissertation on the Antiquities of the two Ancient Ports of Richborough and Sandwich, by the Isle of Tenet, in Kent, by the Rev. John Lewis, printed from the original MS., post 8vo. sewed, 1s. 1851
SELECT FABLES, with Memoir and Catalogue of the Works of Bewick, with several portraits of Bewick, and upwards of 350 woodcuts, 8vo. cloth, 9s., pub. at 15s. 1820
SCOTT. Pedigree of Scott, of Stokoe, in the Parish of Symondburn and County of Northumberland, compiled by William Scott, M.D., with Introduction, Notes, and Continuation, by William Robson Scott, Phil. Doc., post 8vo. cloth, 3s. 6d. 1852
—— The same on large paper, 4to. very few printed, cloth, 7s. ibid.
SCOTLAND. The History and Antiquities of St. Rule's Chapel, in the Monastery of St. Andrew's, in Scotland. To which are added Accounts of the Riding of Parliament, of the Order of the Thistle, and of the Regalia of Scotland, 4to. plates, 2s. 6d., pub. at 10s. 6d. 1787
SEPULCHRAL REMINISCENCES OF A MARKET TOWN, as afforded by a List of the Interments within the Wall of the Parish Church of St. Nicholas, Great Yarmouth, collected chiefly from Monuments and Gravestones still remaining, by Dawson Turner, Esq., F R.S., &c., 8vo. pedigrees of the Cory, Englaced, Ferrier, Ives, Lacon, Manby, Palgrave, and Pether Families, cloth, 4s., pub. at 6s. 1848
CHARLTON (Edward) on the Sepulchral Slabs existing in the Counties of Northumberland and Durham, 8vo. plates, sewed, 1s. 6d.
SINCLAIR. The Correspondence of the Rt. Hon. Sir John Sinclair, Bart., with Reminiscences of the most Distinguished Characters who have appeared in Great Britain, &c., during the last 50 years, 2 vols. thick 8vo. portraits and facsimiles of 200 autographs, bds. 5s. 6d. 1831
SIR EGERTON BRYDGES. Human Fate, and an Address to the Poets Wordsworth and Southey, Poems by the late Sir Egerton Brydges, 8vo. privately printed, 2s. 1848
SOMERSET. Topographical Notes respecting Balls, Wells, Glastonbury, Taunton, &c., by Jeremiah Millés, P.A.S., &c., post 8vo. sewed, 1s. 1851
SPORTING. A short Treatise on the Sportsman's Friend, or the Farmer's Footman, 12mo. copperplate and woodcuts by Thomas Bewick, sewed, very scarce, 3s. 1801
STAINBOROUGH AND ROCKLEY, their Historical Associations and Rural Attractions, by the Author of "Village Rambles," foolscap 8vo. woodcuts, stiff wrapper, 1s. or neat in cloth, 1s. 6d.
SERIES of Eighteen Views in the County of Cheshire, 4to. 5s. 1852
HEARNE'S Views in Cheshire, oblong folio, fine original impressions, SCARCE, 6s. 6d. 1810
KING'S Vale Royal of England, or County Palatine of Chester Illustrated, abridged with Notes by Thomas Hughes, Esq., post 8vo. plates, cloth, 6s.; or large paper, 4to., only 50 copies printed, 12s. 1852
AUNGIER'S History and Antiquities of Syon Monastery, the Parish of Isleworth, and Chapelry of Hounslow, very thick 8vo. plates, &c., bds. 8s., pub. at 21s. 1840
AUTOBIOGRAPHY of William Stout of Lancaster, a Member of the Society of Friends, 1665 to 1752, edited by J. Harland, Esq., 8vo. portrait, cloth, 4s. 6d. 1851
POLWHELE'S (R.) Essay on Marriage, Adultery, and Divorce, post 8vo. bds. SCARCE, 2s. 6d., pub. at 5s. 1823
HUTTON'S (Wm.) Description of Blackpool in Lancashire, 8vo. SCARCE, 1s. 6d. 1817
COLLECTIONS relative to Claims at the Coronations, from that of Richard II., 8vo. bds. 2s. 1838
MATON'S (Dr. E.) Natural History of Part of Wiltshire, 8vo. 1s. 6d. 1843
JONES'S Botanical Tour in Parts of Devon and Cornwall, 12mo. bds. SCARCE, 1s. 6d. 1820
PULMAN'S Rustic Sketches, being Rhymes on Angling, in the West of England Dialect, with Notes and Glossary, post 8vo. cloth, 3s. 6d.; or large paper, only 15 printed, cloth, 7s. 1853
CHERRY AND VIOLET, a Tale of the Great Plague, by the Author of Mary Powell, small 8vo, beautifully printed, bound in cloth, in the antique style, 6s., sells for 7s. 6d.
NATURAL HISTORY of Birds, Quadrupeds, Fishes, Reptiles, Serpents, and Insects, 7 small books, 18mo., cuts by Bewick, SCARCE, 5s.
DANBY'S (William, of Swinton Park, Yorkshire) Thoughts on Various Subjects, post 8vo. bds. 3s., pub. at 7s. 6d. 1831
—— Extracts from Young's Night Thoughts, and from Cicero's Dialogues, with Observations thereon, post 8vo. bds. 3s., pub. at 7s. 6d. 1832
—— Extracts from and Observations on Cicero's Dialogues, 8vo. bds. 2s. 1829

G. BRANDON, Printer, French Horn Yard, 83, High Holborn.

C031716189

RETURN **CIRCULATION DEPARTMENT**
TO ➡ 202 Main Library

LOAN PERIOD 1 **HOME USE**	2	3
4	5	6

ALL BOOKS MAY BE RECALLED AFTER 7 DAYS

1-month loans may be renewed by calling 642-3405
1-year loans may be recharged by bringing the books to the Circulation Desk
Renewals and recharges may be made 4 days prior to due date

DUE AS STAMPED BELOW

JUL 7 1984	
JUN 7 1984	

UNIVERSITY OF CALIFORNIA, BERKELEY
FORM NO. DD6, 60m, 1/83   BERKELEY, CA 94720

CPSIA information can be obtained
at www.ICGtesting.com
Printed in the USA
LVHW041401110219
607139LV00038B/2138/P